TIME FOR
CHANGE

4 **Essential Skills for Transformational School and District Leaders**

ANTHONY MUHAMMAD

LUIS F. CRUZ

Solution Tree | Press

555 North Morton Street
Bloomington, IN 47404
800.733.6786 (toll free) / 812.336.7700
FAX: 812.336.7790

email: info@SolutionTree.com
SolutionTree.com

Visit **go.SolutionTree.com/leadership** to download the free reproducibles in this book.

Printed in the United States of America

Library of Congress Cataloging-in-Publication Data

Names: Muhammad, Anthony, author. | Cruz, Luis F., author.
Title: Time for change : four essential skills for transformational school
   and district leaders / Anthony Muhammad and Luis F. Cruz.
Description: Bloomington, IN : Solution Tree Press, [2019] | Includes
   bibliographical references and index.
Identifiers: LCCN 2018045812 | ISBN 9781942496151 (perfect bound)
Subjects: LCSH: Educational leadership. | Educational change. | School
   environment. | School administrators--Professional relationships.
Classification: LCC LB2806 .M74 2019 | DDC 371.2--dc23 LC record available at https://
lccn.loc.gov/2018045812

Solution Tree
Jeffrey C. Jones, CEO
Edmund M. Ackerman, President

Solution Tree Press
President and Publisher: Douglas M. Rife
Associate Publisher: Sarah Payne-Mills
Art Director: Rian Anderson
Managing Production Editor: Kendra Slayton
Senior Production Editor: Suzanne Kraszewski
Senior Editor: Amy Rubenstein
Copy Editor: Jessi Finn
Proofreader: Sarah Ludwig
Cover Designer: Rian Anderson
Editorial Assistant: Sarah Ludwig

Acknowledgments

I would like to acknowledge Richard and Rebecca DuFour for their tremendous impact on me as an educator, consultant, author, and human being. Their spirits were larger than life, and I pledge that I will do all that I can to carry on their legacy and continue to inspire, enlighten, and uplift educators all over the world.

I would also like to acknowledge the impact and influence of Robert Eaker. He has, and continues to be, a great influence on my work and our thinking. I would also like to acknowledge the hard work and dedication of the Solution Tree staff. I appreciate everything that you do to advance my work! A special shout-out goes to the PLC Associates who continue to enlighten me and stimulate the topics and insights that extend and improve my work. I would like to welcome Dr. Luis Cruz into the circle of authors. I pray that this is just the first of many books to come!

Finally, I would like to acknowledge and thank my wife (Dronda Muhammad), my mother (Anna Nelson), my children, and my entire family for their support and love. You give my life purpose, meaning, and direction. You are truly the wind beneath my wings!

—Anthony Muhammad

I would like to acknowledge "Ricardo" and Rebecca DuFour for allowing me years ago to join their amazing team of educators who collectively work tirelessly to influence learning for students around the world. Your influence optimized my abilities as an educator and human being. I miss you every day and have no doubt you are both collaboratively building PLCs in heaven. I am honored to continue the work you initiated for as long as God allows.

I would like to acknowledge and thank my beautiful wife and best friend (principal extraordinaire in her own right), Pamela Cruz, and my three daughters, Marina,

Anali, and Maya, for their continuous unconditional love and support. To my parents, Felipe and Gladys Cruz, who raised me with a growth mindset: *muchas gracias, Mami and Papi!* It worked! To my other mom (my mother-in-law) who, thank goodness, lives with us: I thank you for the tremendous amount of support you give our home that allows me to travel and interact with educators all over the world.

A special thank-you to my friend Richard Noblett who encouraged me to believe I could make a positive difference in the lives of hardworking educators. Thank you to Jeff Jones, Shannon Ritz, Claudia Wheatley, Douglas Rife, and the superb team from Solution Tree for allowing me to be a part of an amazing organization that is transforming lives around the world: it is truly an honor!

Thank you to my personal editor, Rachel Richards from Orange Glen High School in Escondido, California, for her patience reviewing the written work of this grown-up English learner. I appreciate your patience and gentle feedback with my prepositional phrase issue.

To the amazing and talented Mike Mattos and Ken Williams for your willingness to share your brilliance and passion with me from the get-go. I am a better consultant and presenter today because of you, my brothers for life.

Finally, thank you to my "brother from another mother," Anthony Muhammad, for literally taking me under your wings over a decade ago and sharing your wisdom and genius with me with no strings attached. I am grateful to the Lord above for allowing our paths to cross as I am a better educator and person today because of your influence in my life. I look forward to a lifetime of friendship.

—Luis F. Cruz

Visit **go.SolutionTree.com/leadership** to download the free reproducibles in this book.

Table of Contents

Chapter 5

Getting Results: Collecting the Return on Investment **83**

Chapter 6

Tying It All Together **109**

Afterword: Final Thoughts **127**

References and Resources **129**

Index **135**

About the Authors

 **Anthony Muhammad, PhD,** is a much sought-after educational consultant. A practitioner for nearly twenty years, he has served as a middle school teacher, assistant principal, and principal and as a high school principal. His Transforming School Culture framework explores the root causes of staff resistance to change.

Anthony's tenure as a practitioner has earned him several awards as both a teacher and a principal. His most notable accomplishment came as principal of Levey Middle School in Southfield, Michigan, a National School of Excellence, where student proficiency on state assessments more than doubled in five years. Anthony and the staff at Levey used the Professional Learning Communities (PLCs) at Work® process for school improvement, and the school has been recognized in several videos and articles as a model high-performing PLC.

As a researcher, Anthony has published articles in several publications in both the United States and Canada. He is author of *Transforming School Culture: How to Overcome Staff Division*; *The Will to Lead, the Skill to Teach: Transforming Schools at Every Level*; and *Overcoming the Achievement Gap Trap: Liberating Mindsets to Effect Change* and a contributor to *The Collaborative Administrator*.

To learn more about Anthony's work, visit New Frontier 21 (www.newfrontier21 .com), or follow @newfrontier21 on Twitter.

 **Luis F. Cruz, PhD,** is former principal of Baldwin Park High School and Holland Middle School, located east of Los Angeles, California. He has been a teacher at the elementary level and administrator at the elementary, middle, and high school levels. Luis is an educational consultant who presents throughout the United States on PLCs, school culture, the role of school leadership teams, RTI, and the conditions needed for students and parents learning English as a second language to be academically successful.

In 2007, Luis led a collective effort to secure a $250,000 grant for Baldwin Park from the California Academic Partnership Program for the purpose of effectively utilizing courageous leadership to promote a more equitable and effective organization.

Since becoming a public school educator, Luis has won the New Teacher of the Year, Teacher of the Year, and Administrator of the Year awards and other community leadership awards. He and a committee of teacher leaders at Baldwin Park High School received the California School Boards Association's prestigious Golden Bell Award for significantly closing the achievement gap between the general student population and students learning English as a second language.

As a recipient of the Hispanic Border Leadership Institute's fellowship for doctoral studies, a fellowship focused on increasing the number of Latino leaders with doctorates, he earned a doctorate in institutional leadership and policy studies from the University of California, Riverside. He earned an associate's degree from Mt. San Antonio Community College, a bachelor's degree from California State University, Fullerton, and a master's degree from Claremont Graduate University.

To learn more about Luis's work, follow @lcruzconsulting on Twitter.

To book Anthony Muhammad or Luis F. Cruz for professional development, contact pd@SolutionTree.com.

Introduction

The most vital assets in any organization are the human resources, and the leader is responsible for managing these resources. The task of cultivating, organizing, and motivating people to improve an organization's productivity holds much importance, especially for school leaders, who seek improvement to ensure that students grow, develop, and reach their maximum potential, the key to a community's prosperity. Leading school improvement is serious business, indeed!

Research shows a general consensus that schools can improve, but how to improve schools remains a topic of much research and heated debate both politically and intellectually. On one hand, many argue that school systems should take a corporate approach; they should use data to monitor performance, rewarding the productive educators and removing the ineffective ones. The other school of thought suggests that leaders should provide educators with a supportive and nurturing environment, trust them with a high degree of professional autonomy, and assume that they will make good, professional decisions. In this book, we argue that school leadership has much more complexity than either of these two approaches; leaders must do more than simply order change or nurture a warm organizational climate and hope that people will change. Effective school leaders must develop specific skills—a balance of both having assertiveness and encouraging autonomy—to engage those they lead in the change process.

Richard DuFour and Michael Fullan (2013) perfectly sum up our argument in the following passage from their book *Cultures Built to Last: Systemic PLCs at Work*®:

> How should leaders engage people in the complex process of cultural change? Should they be *tight*—assertive, issuing top-down directives that mandate change? Or should they be *loose*—merely encouraging people to engage in the change process, but leaving participation optional? The challenge at all

levels of the system is to navigate this apparent dichotomy and find the appropriate balance between tight and loose, between assertiveness and autonomy. If we know anything about change, it is that ordering people to change doesn't work, nor does leaving them alone. (p. 33)

The delicate balance between *loose* and *tight*, as DuFour and Fullan (2013) describe it, requires that a leader have a comprehensive set of leadership skills. Without these skills, trying to differentiate between the right time to nurture and the right time to demand performance can lead current and aspiring school leaders down a slippery slope. People cannot logically expect that this collection of delicate skills would come naturally to everyone seeking to lead schools. In fact, we contend that people rarely have the instincts necessary to naturally strike this balance, and without proper guidance, every school would need a superhero to create the conditions for improvement. Fullan (2003) acknowledges that the goal should be to make leadership "more exciting and doable. It cannot require superwomen and supermen or moral martyrs because, if it does, we will never get the numbers necessary to make a system difference" (p. xv).

Our goal with this book is to provide leaders with a logical and duplicable process so that anyone who wants to become an effective school leader has a road map for success. We begin by exploring what we know about good leadership.

Leadership as a Skill

Leadership represents the ability to use influence to improve organizational productivity. Leadership is not a position; it is a set of actions that positively shape the climate and culture of the working environment. In essence, leadership is a verb, not a noun. We know a good leader is present when those whom he or she influences have become more effective and productive at their given task because of the impact of the leader. Consider this: most would agree that a reading teacher lacks effectiveness if his or her students don't improve their reading skills after being exposed to the practices and influence of a reading teacher. Wouldn't the same standard apply to a school or district leader? He or she is not a successful leader if those he or she leads do not succeed. For this reason, isolating and evaluating individual teachers as the sole indicator for school progress, using their students' test scores to determine success or failure, is doomed to fail as a public policy and school-improvement method. The teacher does not work on an island; the teacher is a product of his or her leaders, just as the teacher influences a student. In fact, no one truly works in isolation. Educators are a part of an intricate web, each contributing to the success or failure of their system. All educators are leaders, yet they all need leadership. The question each educator should ask becomes, "What responsibility do I have for influencing and improving those I have to guide?"

In a school, productivity is measured in terms of this influence and improvement in both student learning and personal growth. Productive schools shape the future in positive ways. Education is a high-stakes business, not because of a ranking or accountability rating given by a state or government agency, but because educators only get thirteen years to help shape the future of young human beings. This shaping process requires profound care and skill. This makes school leadership one of the most critical positions in a progressive society.

Too often, people assume that because someone has shown promise or experienced success in a particular area, he or she has the ability to guide others to that same level of greatness. This is simply an inaccurate assumption. Andrew Munro (2005) warns:

> Wrapping up attributes, behaviours, tasks and outcomes into a package of competency dimensions might seem an economical way of summarising leadership and management requirements, but by bundling cause and consequence there is a risk of confusing who is currently effective (displaying the achievement of outcomes) from who might be effective in the future (evidence of those attributes predictive of outcomes). (p. 65)

Schools cannot ensure effective school leadership by simply promoting a good teacher to the role of principal or promoting a good principal to the role of superintendent. The skills required to lead other people differ from those personal and professional skills required to perform other tasks. In 2002, the National Association of Secondary School Principals (NASSP) reported that by 2012, 40 percent of the United States' principals would retire, and qualified candidates would not replace most of them. We are now years beyond that stark warning. The NASSP (2002) report also notes that few school districts have structured recruitment programs that systematically seek out the best principal candidates, or implement training programs that grow future leaders.

Unfortunately, the crisis predicted in 2002 was even worse than anticipated. In a stunning report titled *Churn: The High Cost of Principal Turnover*, the School Leaders Network (2014) confirms that 25 percent of principals leave their post each year and 50 percent leave after three years. That same report also highlights the impact that principal turnover and effectiveness have on students. It concludes that a 10 percent drop in principal turnover in high-poverty communities, coupled with district investment in principal effectiveness, would translate to an increase of $30,024.07 in lifetime earnings for students enrolled in those schools (School Leaders Network, 2014). Therefore, it is imperative that school systems recruit and retain leaders who understand how to lead and sustain school improvement. This requires that school and district leaders possess a set of diverse skills that can impact both the technical and cultural dimensions of organizational change.

Technical change involves the manipulation of policies, structures, and practices. Organizations really need this form of change, but when used exclusively, it ignores very important aspects of organizational reform (Muhammad, 2009). *Cultural change* refers to addressing the beliefs, values, motivations, habits, and behaviors of the people who work within the organization. People often overlook this form of change because it is challenging and complex (Muhammad, 2009). In this book, we will establish that changing the culture of an organization is essential to improving outcomes, and it provides the context to make technical innovation effective. Technically savvy but culturally ineffective leaders will find little success in transforming schools.

Human beings are complex, so leaders need a skill set as diverse as human beings themselves in order to cultivate better practice. To begin our discussion of the skills that effective change leaders require, we first look at the transformational leadership model and what it means to become a transformational leader.

Transformational Leadership

James MacGregor Burns (1978) originally introduced the transformational leadership model in a book titled *Leadership*. Burns (1978) describes *transformational leadership* as a process where "leaders and followers raise one another to higher levels of motivation and morality" (p. 20). The clarity and specifics of this model have advanced since he first introduced it in 1978. His original model provided a paradigm for transformational influence but very few specifics. Bernard M. Bass (1985) significantly contributed to the study of this model when he introduced eight characteristics of transformational leadership.

1. Model integrity and fairness.
2. Set clear goals.

3. Have high expectations.

4. Encourage others.

5. Provide support and recognition.

6. Stir people's emotions.

7. Encourage people to look beyond their self-interest.

8. Inspire people to reach for the improbable.

A scholarly paper that Langston University (2016) published, titled *Transformational Leadership*, includes the most compelling and vivid description of this form of leadership that we have found:

> Transformational leadership is defined as a leadership approach that causes change in individuals and social systems. In its ideal form, it creates valuable and positive change in the followers with the end goal of developing followers into leaders. Enacted in its authentic form, transformational leadership enhances the motivation, morale and performance of followers through a variety of mechanisms. (p. 1)

We believe that schools will have the best chance to significantly impact student outcomes if they develop transformational leaders—leaders who understand that their behavior significantly contributes to their schools, districts, families, communities, and world. Leadership is serious business; an ineffective leader can make a lasting negative impression while an effective leader can positively impact lives for generations. We believe that every school and every district deserves transformational leaders.

The evolving definition of a transformational leader has led us to a question: What skills must a leader possess to positively influence those who are subject to his or her leadership? The previous works have heavily described the outcomes but lightly described the specific skills needed to achieve them. Because effective change leaders are not born, but rather evolve from experience and training, we seek to provide a concrete and duplicable guide for becoming a transformational leader. We don't need superheroes to get this right. We need to focus on four essential skills that transformational leaders need—skills that focus on the *why*, the *who*, and the *how* of change—so that leaders and those they lead can ultimately *do* the change, making it a reality.

1. **Leaders must effectively communicate the rationale—the *why* of the work:** People tend to resist change to practice and lack motivation to improve when leaders have not skillfully communicated the rationale or case for improvement. To embrace a vision, people have to clearly understand the vision and feel personally compelled to contribute to the vision.

2. **Leaders must effectively establish trust—the *who* of the work:** A transformational leader needs the very essential ability to connect with others' emotions. Facts and objective evidence alone do not inspire people; people need to connect with their leader on a personal level and know that their leader has not just an intellectual connection but also an ethical connection to their purpose.

3. **Leaders must effectively build capacity—the *how* of the work:** People will more willingly take a risk and try a new idea if leaders have prepared them professionally. Leaders must invest in training, resources, and time if they want educators to enthusiastically embrace new ideas and practices.

4. **Leaders must get results—the *do* of the work:** Ultimately, improvement cannot be optional. A transformational leader must skillfully assess and meet the needs of those he or she leads, but eventually, he or she has to demand full participation in the change and improvement process.

In addition, we want to clarify that transformational school leadership is not only synonymous with administration. Teachers, counselors, and classified staff (secretaries, custodians, and paraprofessionals) may actively help promote change initiatives that benefit a school's core purpose. Throughout this book, we provide a variety of experiences in the form of scenarios that leaders—not just administrators—might find themselves in, along with skills and strategies to utilize during the change process.

Chapter Overviews

We have designed this book to serve as a practical, research-based tool for anyone looking to improve his or her leadership skills to achieve more favorable results. We will examine research on effective leadership, current and past obstacles to progressive change, and philosophical and concrete tools designed to maximize educational professionals' performance.

Chapter 1 provides a theoretical case for transformational leadership. We will examine the history of trying to effect change in schools by looking at the scholarship and the methods and determine why they failed to achieve the desired change. We establish our model's mechanics as we explore the advantages of taking a balanced approach to change by blending the principles of support and accountability. A leader's ability to address the why, the who, and the how and then do makes up the core of the transformational leadership concept.

Chapter 2 addresses leaders' need to communicate the rationale—the why. Communication involves more than the simple transfer of information. When leaders address the why with their followers, they connect to the rational side of human nature essential in the quest to improve performance and outcomes. It is the ability to create, articulate, and inspire other people to invest in an organizational vision larger than themselves that makes a leader transformational.

Chapter 3 addresses leaders' need to build trust—the who. In this chapter, we examine the development of a leader's ability to successfully create meaningful professional relationships. A leader must have the ability to connect with human nature's emotional side in the quest to improve performance and outcomes. Sometimes, people are motivated by a change concept because it resonates intellectually with them, while others commit to a change because they believe in the person who leads the change. The ability to communicate without the ability to appeal to people emotionally and build trust leads to only partial transformation.

Chapter 4 addresses leaders' need to build capacity—the how. A leader must know how to diagnose his or her followers' professional and material needs in the quest to improve performance and outcomes. No matter how much a person recognizes the need to change and connects with his or her colleagues in a deep, emotional way, he or she can't effectively participate in change without the skills to execute the practice and the resources to do so successfully. Leaders need to engage in capacity building to close the skill gaps that cause some people to disengage with the change process.

Chapter 5 addresses leaders' need to get results—the do. After a leader makes significant investments in the needs of the organization's members, a moment of truth occurs where preparation meets execution. A leader who does not have the courage to demand execution just turns a vision into a suggestion. A good leader must anticipate that even with the sincerest of support efforts, a small party of individuals will probably only respond to authority. At that moment, a transformational leader has to be willing to demand compliance.

Chapter 6 further discusses the components of the transformational leadership model by tying them all together with tips for implementation. We provide a call to action and challenge school leaders to move from talking about substantive change to creating a plan that leads people through this process.

Throughout the book, we provide scenarios constructed from the experiences of real school leaders along with tools for reflection so that you can practice thinking and acting like a transformational leader. Like any other skill, leadership has to be practiced, so we have described and highlighted some compelling dilemmas faced by real leaders. These exercises will allow you to sharpen your skills so you can avoid making mistakes in real time with real people.

Conclusion

Past school leadership models have lacked balance and the proper insight into human motivation, which has resulted in little change and little progress in raising overall student achievement and closing academic achievement gaps. The need for quality education is dire. By the year 2020, 65 percent of American jobs will require some form of postsecondary education (Carnevale, Smith, & Strohl, 2010). The evidence from reliable achievement data demonstrates that U.S. schools have not academically accelerated students who live in poverty and the United States' black and Latino students to meet this job market's demands. A 2014 U.S. Department of Education report finds the following regarding U.S. schools.

> ▸ Among high schools serving the highest percentage of African American and Latino students, one in three do not offer a single chemistry course, and one in four do not offer a course more advanced than algebra 1.

> ▸ In schools that offer gifted and talented programs, African American and Latino students represent 40 percent of students, but only 26 percent of those students enroll in such programs.

> ▸ African American students, Latino students, and students living below the national poverty line attend schools with higher concentrations of first-year teachers than do middle-class white students.

▸ African American students are suspended and expelled from school at a rate more than three times as high as white students (16 percent versus 5 percent).

These data reinforce the fact that school leadership, at every level, needs to improve. Student academic success and skill development are matters of survival for many, especially in a world that is quickly moving away from the industrial model into a knowledge-based economy. The needs of society are changing faster than many schools' ability to create positive momentum, especially for our most vulnerable populations. If effective leadership is judged by positive impact on performance, these data suggest that there is a huge need for positive influence and change in our school systems. Improving the skill and effectiveness of leadership is essential in the quest to provide every student with a quality and useful education. As we work with school leaders, we do not observe a lack of sincerity and desire to improve the effectiveness of their environments. What we observe are sincere, hardworking people who lack an understanding of how to properly cultivate an environment of change. We believe that the transformational leadership model, and the essential skills attached to this model, is the best solution to this problem.

1

Finding Balance for Systems Change

If there is one thing people can likely all agree on, it is that change is hard. Whether individually battling a personal vice, like smoking, or striving to change other long-held habits, people find it difficult to will themselves to abandon an unproductive behavior for a more productive behavior, even if they have overwhelming evidence for change. Schools face an even more daunting, complex challenge than individual change—systems change, a challenge that many school and system leaders have failed to meet.

Daniel H. Pink (2011) writes, "Too many organizations—not just companies, but governments and nonprofits as well—still operate from assumptions about human potential and individual performance that are outdated, unexamined, and rooted more in folklore than in science" (p. 9). The challenge of change is tough enough with the right skills and research-based strategies, but when a system operates from its own conjecture, folklore, and gut instincts, it makes the task nearly impossible. Pink (2011) points out that gut instincts lead to one of two very ineffective assumptions.

1. People are motivated through force—the stick approach.

2. People are motivated through incentives—the carrot approach.

He notes that both assumptions are incorrect because people have much more complexity and nuance than their fears or material desires.

Educational leadership practices and educational policies reflect this lack of insight into the complexity of human nature. Richard DuFour (2015) eloquently dismantles these incorrect assumptions and ineffective policies and practices in his book *In Praise of American Educators: And How They Can Become Even Better*. DuFour (2015) documents seven assumptions, which have roots in neither fact nor science, that continue to guide change efforts in U.S. public schools. These assumptions have not worked or even come close to changing schools for the better.

1. Charter schools will improve other public schools.

2. Providing vouchers to send students to other public or private schools will improve public schools.

3. More testing means more accountability.

4. Intensive supervision and evaluation will lead to the dismissal of ineffective teachers.

5. Value-based testing provides a valid way to reward effective teachers and dismiss ineffective teachers.

6. Merit pay will improve teaching and therefore improve schools.

7. Closing low-performing schools will improve remaining schools.

Schools cannot continue to support such assumptions and go down the same path of sticks and carrots (punishments and rewards). These old and tired strategies just don't work! We need to empower a generation of leaders who truly understand the science of human motivation to bring out the best in the professionals who serve our students. Unfortunately, as the history of education in the United States shows, changing education is easier said than done.

In this chapter, we examine change in education and change in school culture, how balanced leadership is needed for change, and the three investments and one condition leaders must make to develop intrinsic motivation for change in those they lead.

Change in Education

Schools are not much different than they were in the late 19th century. Many staples that characterized education in the 19th century have gone unchallenged in the 20th and 21st centuries. These conditions include the following (Tyack & Cuban, 1995).

▶ The teacher is the content expert and directs students' learning.

▶ Students assimilate to the teacher's educational and behavioral expectations and receive positive feedback for behavioral assimilation and successful regurgitation of facts.

▶ Instructional autonomy is considered a teacher's professional right, and that right typically goes unchallenged, regardless of evidence of teacher effectiveness.

Not only do many school conditions remain the same for students, but the personal and professional experiences that teachers encounter add yet another layer of challenge.

In his groundbreaking book *Schoolteacher: A Sociological Study*, Dan C. Lortie (1975) uncovers some obvious barriers to change and helps us understand why change in education is so difficult. In fact, he declares that schools present more challenges than any other institution. Schools go largely unchanged, according to Lortie (1975), because of two major factors.

1. The traditional system has socialized educators into its standard practices and expectations since they themselves were in kindergarten, and their teacher preparation programs reinforced those same values. Lortie (1975) refers to this as the *apprenticeship of observation*. People who have never had exposure to an alternative find it difficult to envision change.

2. The vast majority of educators performed at a relatively high level as students, so they have not had enough adverse experiences to motivate them to advocate for systems change. In fact, Lortie (1975) argues, they would more likely protect the system than deconstruct it.

Colin Lacey, a contemporary of Lortie, validated Lortie's conclusions in 1977 with the first printing of his book *The Socialization of Teachers*. In a 2012 edition of the same book, Lacey concludes that the exposure to school and educational norms at a young age socializes teachers to acquire the same dispositions and paradigms today that Lortie observed in 1975.

The challenges to achieving substantive school change are real and intimidating. Not only must educators face a changing job market that requires students to acquire more skills, but leaders have to combat a system that has not changed much since the late 19th century. Also, leaders have to confront the hardened expectations of educators and parents who were socialized in the system that leaders seek to change. Schools have to find a better way to prepare new and current leaders for these challenges, or they will continue to recycle the same ineffective methods of the past. We propose that leaders should start by changing school culture.

Change in School Culture

We have established that schools are not wired for change. This is not a recent development; it is built right into the DNA of the educational system. To make an impact on this profession, leaders need to understand culture and know how to change it. Terrence E. Deal and Kent D. Peterson (1999) are widely credited for shaping the study of school culture. These authors describe school culture as a school's collective norms, values, beliefs, rituals, symbols, celebrations, and stories that make up its *persona*. They also provide a prototype of the optimal school culture, which they call a *healthy school culture*.

A healthy school culture produces a professional environment in which educators unwaveringly believe that all students have the ability to achieve academic and social success, and they overtly and covertly communicate that expectation to others. Educators in these environments are willing to create policies, practices, and procedures that align with their beliefs and are rooted in their confidence in universal student achievement. To paraphrase, educators in a healthy school culture believe that all students can excel, and they willingly challenge and change their own practices to meet that end. This is the environment necessary to create the required change that can prepare students for the 21st century's skill-based job market. We argue that an educational leader's inability to create a healthy school culture is the primary reason school performance goes unchanged or declines and the achievement gap remains wide.

John Hattie (2012) has measured the impact of many important factors that predict and influence student learning. Those factors include environmental, economic, professional, and cultural factors. In his book *Visible Learning for Teachers: Maximizing Impact on Learning*, Hattie (2012) identifies the top-three factors, which all relate to culture and belief in or prediction of student achievement.

1. Teacher estimates of achievement

2. Collective teacher efficacy

3. Student estimates of achievement or self-reported grades

Hattie's (2012) findings show that students will learn more and have more success in an environment in which all educators believe that the students can learn at high levels. Those educators work together to convince students that they can achieve the lofty academic goals that their teachers set for them. A leader who understands how to cultivate this type of culture will place a school clearly on the path to improvement and sustainable growth. The skills necessary to create a healthy culture greatly differ from those on the ineffective and destructive path to change, which the field of education has experienced in the past.

A healthy culture operates from two important assumptions. The first expects that everyone within the organization believes that students can and will learn at high levels. The second assumption is that the educators who work within a healthy culture are willing to change or adjust their behavior based on objective evidence about student growth and development. Coupling lofty expectations for student success with a willingness to change practice based on those expectations creates a very effective and balanced school culture.

Balanced Leadership

Past approaches to systemic change have lacked balance. For example, the federal educational policy No Child Left Behind (NCLB, 2002) demanded that schools achieve a standard of annual academic performance on state assessments in both mathematics and reading (adequate yearly progress, or AYP) or face state and federal government sanctions. This sent a simple message: improve or face punishment (a stick approach). This approach certainly got people's attention, but it did not stimulate the level of moral and personal commitment necessary for deep change. This totally coercive method led to states lowering their academic testing standards so they could prevent schools from receiving the label of *failing* (Peterson & Hess, 2008). And some states created loopholes in their accountability systems to omit counting students with certain risk factors so that schools could falsely boost their test scores (Dizon, Feller, & Bass, 2006). Ultimately, this punitive approach led to nearly net-zero student achievement growth between 2002 and 2013 (Ravitch, 2013).

President Barack Obama's administration tried a different approach to improving schools in 2009. Though it did not eliminate NCLB as a federal policy, it allowed states leeway on some provisions and offered them incentives through federal programs like Race to the Top to reward schools into improving (U.S. Department of Education, 2013). Many states offered teachers merit pay for better student test scores and created outcome-based teacher evaluation systems to reward effective teachers financially (a carrot approach). This type of approach might create short-term commitment or interest until the educator no longer considers the incentive a priority.

The preliminary evidence from the shift from stick to carrot reveals that the latter approach has not effected tangible student learning outcomes much more than the former approach, especially as it pertains to closing the achievement gap for students at risk (Lee, 2014). Decision makers and policymakers have not learned that human beings are much more complex and nuanced than these policies, aimed at stimulating motivation to improve performance, suppose.

A lack of balance in leadership approach is the biggest factor in leadership ineffectiveness (Bass, 1981). We propose that transformational leaders must strike a balance between the important elements of focusing on the task and focusing on relationships and between providing support and requiring accountability.

Task and Relationship Balance

Leadership researcher and pioneer Bernard M. Bass (1981) felt that the most critical mistake most leaders make is placing too much emphasis either on the task at hand or on relationships with others. Bass (1981) describes leaders as tending to be either *task focused* (emphasizing rules and procedures for getting the task done) or *follower focused* (emphasizing concern for people).

Task-Focused Leadership

A task-focused leader initiates structure, provides vital information, determines what people should do, issues the rules, promises rewards for compliance, and threatens punishment for disobedience. The task-focused leader uses his or her power to obtain compliance. Task-focused leadership produces some benefits.

▶ Clarity of focus

▶ Outcomes orientation

▶ Predictability

▶ Clear expectations

▶ Strong protocol and procedures

Task-focused leadership will also generate some disadvantages.

▶ Fear of failure or lack of job security

▶ Alienation

▶ Lack of professional creativity

▶ Lack of commitment

▶ Passive-aggressive behavior and informal protest

Follower-Focused Leadership

A follower-focused leader solicits advice, opinions, and information from those he or she leads and checks decisions or shares decision making with them. The follower-focused leader uses his or her power to set the constraints within which he or she encourages followers to help decide the organization's course or direction. Follower-focused leadership produces some benefits.

▶ A sense of appreciation and respect

▶ Multiple perspectives

▶ Fostered collaboration

▶ Shared sense of ownership

▶ Reflective practice

Follower-focused leadership will also generate some disadvantages.

▶ Slow progress

▶ Philosophical conflicts

▶ Constant change

▶ Disorganized systems

▶ Lack of focus

Bass (1981) concludes that leaders must balance emphasis on the task and emphasis on the human relationships. A one-sided approach would meet some needs, while simultaneously creating problems because of unmet needs. The goal of leadership is to build the organization's human capital—to transform the relationship between leader and followers so that unity of purpose and mutually shared goals energize and motivate participants. Transformational leadership is based on the conviction that the people in the organization constitute resources rich in ideas, knowledge, creativity, and energy, and leaders can fully tap into their power only by creating organizational environments that are motivating, inclusive, organized, and focused on outcomes.

We argue that developing the human being (relationship) provides the context for the important job of demanding performance (task). In fact, we believe that leaders cannot ethically demand performance without first preparing people for the task that they expect them to perform. To attain the level of balance that Bass (1981) advocates, leaders must strike a profound balance between support and accountability.

Support and Accountability Balance

To simplify the concept of *support and accountability balance*, we describe support as an *investment* and accountability as a *return on investment*. In the world of finance, an investor would understand that it is very illogical to expect a return on investment if he or she made no initial investment. He or she would see gathering the capital to invest in a business, stock, or venture as a very simple and logical prerequisite to entering the world of financial investment. We will prove that it should not shock leaders that they do not reap a dividend when they make no real investment in their employees and simply demand performance.

The first job of a transformational leader is to examine how much investment he or she needs to make in order to receive a substantial return. We believe that school employees require three essential human investments or supports in order to improve practices and outcomes: (1) communication, (2) trust, and (3) capacity building. These supports align with the skills a transformational leader must possess that we outline in chapters 2–4 of this book.

Conversely, we believe that a leader who simply analyzes needs and makes investments without any expectation of improvement has only wasted time and resources and will not witness substantive improvement. An investor who works hard to gather and invest capital but does not expect a high rate of return on investment has wasted substantial time and energy. School leaders who create positive relationships, solicit input, communicate priorities, and provide training for improvement but do not articulate higher performance expectations and do not monitor improvement have wasted substantial time and energy. The second job of a transformational leader, then, is to demand accountability. This aligns with the fourth skill we outline in chapter 5 (page 83)—that leaders must get results.

In order to get results, transformational leaders must also understand the dynamics of motivation and resistance to change. Leaders may find this hard to accept, but most resistance to change is a rational response to ineffective leadership.

Motivation and Resistance to Change

Leaders often respond to resistance as they would to a negative behavior—they address the behavior without assessing the cause. Most resistance to change manifests a need that a leader has not met, or a critical investment that a leader has neglected. Before a leader can criticize a follower for not embracing a vision or a directive, he or she has to first assess whether he or she has made all the necessary investments to warrant a return on investment. Leaders have to make three non-negotiable investments to create the right conditions for intrinsic motivation for change: (1) cognitive investment, (2) emotional investment, and (3) functional investment. When those three investments fail to stimulate change, a leader can conclude that the resistant behavior has resulted from more personal reasons or an exercise in power. At that point, a leader can fairly conclude that the individual, who has all the tools and opportunities for change, has drawn a line in the sand and challenged the leader's authority. The only conclusion to such a standoff is coercion; the leader has a right to collect the return on his or her investment (the fourth and final condition for intrinsic motivation for change). In the following sections, we describe the three non-negotiable investments and the fourth condition.

Cognitive Investment

When parents reach their wits' end when scolding a teenager who made a poor choice because of peer pressure, they might ask, "If your friend jumped off a bridge, would you do it too?" This common question calls for pragmatism. Parents want their children to use good judgment, gather facts, and come to a rational conclusion. To understand why something is important and reach a logical and beneficial conclusion requires examining evidence, weighing options, and engaging in a dialogue, both internally and externally. We believe that leaders often deny educators these opportunities to logically understand the why of change, and this frustrates them, leading to pessimism and withdrawal from change.

Emotional Investment

Not all experience is good experience. As we will note in chapter 2 (page 23), school leadership has an astronomical turnover rate. When a leader surveys the environment and assesses its readiness for change, he or she has to consider the experiences that educators had with leaders who came before. Ignoring this reality is not wise. Past experiences leave an emotional imprint on a person. This imprint impacts anyone who seeks to enter into a relationship with that person. Would a person be wise to become engaged to a fiancé who has had five divorces in ten years, ignoring how past experiences have shaped the current reality? We believe that most people would say, "No!" Likewise, would a new superintendent be wise to ignore the fact that he or she is a district's third superintendent in five years? Shouldn't he or she consider the effect those previous experiences had on school district employees? Leaders must consider emotions when trying to create intrinsic commitment to change in a staff. When leaders ignore people's emotions and experiences, that alone can stimulate a pessimistic view of change.

Functional Investment

Leaders cannot fairly require someone to complete a task that they have not properly prepared him or her to complete. In our work, we witness many instances where school or district officials introduce significant changes to professional practice and expect that one half-day workshop will sufficiently provide all the skills necessary to perform the newly introduced task. Considering that teachers receive at least four years of university-level practice to simply enter the classroom door, it is unrealistic for leaders to think learning needs stop once they become licensed. Poorly constructed professional learning experiences, inadequate resources, and little time for full implementation can be enough to give teachers a negative view of change.

Return on Investment

If a person clearly understands why change is logical and essential, has trust in leaders, and has received extensive training, adequate practice time, and essential resources to effectively execute the task, all that remains is to complete the task. This moment—when action can take place—marks the tipping point between support and accountability. Once leaders have made their investments, it is perfectly logical to expect a return on those investments. Demanding that a person change for the good of the organization takes courage; leaders must be willing to have some dislike them for the sake of a cause bigger than any individual. Here, the leader protects the organization's heart and soul and draws a line between personal preference and organizational purpose. The willingness to coerce others when faced with illogical resistance solidifies a leader's status as a person of principle. Allowing a few outliers to disrespect the will of the entire organization sends the message that change is a personal choice and, ultimately, that improvement is a choice. A transformational leader does not send this message, because it stifles change.

These investments tie in with the four skills of a transformational leader that we advance in the chapters that follow: (1) communicating the rationale, (2) establishing trust, (3) building capacity, and (4) getting results. Figure 1.1 illustrates this system of four skills.

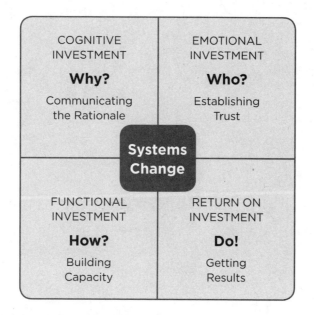

Figure 1.1: The Why? Who? How? Do! model.

Conclusion

In an organization, resistance to change in practice or behavior is a symptom of individual or collective needs not being met. Those needs vary from person to person and from school to school. They include cognitive (why), emotional (who), and functional (how) needs. These needs are rational; they emerge out of negative personal and professional experiences. A perceptive transformational leader knows how to diagnose and respond to rational needs without taking the resistance personally.

While some resist change because of rational needs, others resist change out of an irrational and selfish need for power, without consideration of the impact that it will have on the organization, and ultimately on students. This behavior requires a leader to demand a return on investment and properly exercise leadership authority to ensure compliance without intellectual or emotional consent from the resisting party (do).

In the chapters that follow, we provide deep insight into developing a balanced leadership skill set that will equip leaders to meet these diverse needs.

2

Communicating the Rationale: Building Cognitive Investment

A principal stands before her staff, appearing unsure and apologetic, as she asks teachers to fill out a set of new compliance documents and templates from the central office. This latest mandate requires that teachers document every formal and informal intervention interaction they have with individual students during the course of instruction. The principal hears chatter from the back of the room as teachers ponder the purpose of yet another task that seems meaningless.

The principal reluctantly shares that completion of the task is mandatory and failure to do so will have a negative impact on their formal yearly performance evaluations. The principal appears defeated, and now the staff look defeated. The lack of dialogue and intellectual consent makes the staff feel devalued.

The lack of intellectual synergy and communication in the school has led to a culture of hopelessness and pessimism. This environment is not ripe for improvement. A leader who understands the power of communication could greatly improve the culture and productivity of this school.

As we discussed in chapter 1 (page 11), research and experience have shown that attempting to control others with external forces such as punishments and rewards is an exercise in futility. We argue that a crucial factor in motivating people lies within the individuals themselves. To set the stage for motivating those they lead, transformational leaders create the right environment and seek to critically understand the needs of the organization and motivate others to work together to collaboratively meet those needs.

Psychologist Frederick Herzberg (1966) believes that people's internal capacities, both cognitive and emotional, give rise to feelings, aspirations, perceptions, attitudes, and thoughts that can lead to either motivation or demotivation. Herzberg (1966) states that leaders must recognize human beings as complex and need stimulation on several different levels in order to unleash their followers' intrinsic commitment. When leaders do this, they create conditions that will more likely satisfy followers' internal capacity, thus motivating followers to adopt the organization's goal as their own. Herzberg (1966) calls this type of environment a *growth-enhancing environment*. Such an environment does not require authoritarian mandates to stimulate change; the members of the organization will drive change because of their intrinsic connection to the growth of the organization. Carol Dweck (2006) calls this a *growth mindset*. They will also consider the validity of externally developed innovation as long as it is congruent with organizational needs. In essence, they would view the organization's needs like they would view their own personal needs. In this environment, innovation is not a disruption; it is a necessity.

Transformational leaders also appeal to people's innate drive to understand the world, to make sense of it, to gain control over their lives, and to become increasingly self-directed. This cognitive perception, which world-renowned psychologist Jean Piaget (1977) advanced, assumes that a need for predictability, sensibleness, and logic motivates people when dealing with a vast and diverse world. In essence, a person's need to understand the world and make sense of his or her environment would make him or her gravitate toward regularity, and deep understanding of a task and how it relates to his or her personal needs. Piaget (1977) calls this *equilibration*. If people clearly understand how the tasks that leaders ask them to complete connect to their natural need to solve problems, it will motivate them and make them intensely committed to solving the problem at hand.

Creating a growth-enhancing environment and achieving equilibration both require that leaders answer the question, Why? Asking and answering this question represents one of the most important things a leader can do to create intrinsic commitment to change. In doing so, the leader fulfills followers' cognitive needs by communicating the rationale for change.

Communicating the Rationale as a Leadership Skill

Why? may seem like a very basic question with an easy answer, but the evidence proves that many leaders fail to address it, and failure to do so leads to apathy, disconnection, and resistance. And, in some cases, it leads to followers abandoning the profession of education.

A 2016 Learning Policy Institute report documents that U.S. K–12 schools lose about 8 percent of their workforce every year, and only about one-third of those workers leave the profession because of retirement (Sutcher, Darling-Hammond, & Carver-Thomas, 2016). Nonretirement exits from the teaching profession most prevalently occur due to issues connected to school leadership effectiveness. Teachers who rate their school leadership *ineffective* are twice as likely to leave the profession as those who rate it *effective*. The most dominant factor in whether teachers rated school leadership as effective was decision-making input (Sutcher et al., 2016). Teachers want the opportunity to exchange ideas with leaders and colleagues—to communicate—and rationalize changes in their practice.

The Ken Blanchard Companies (2016), led by internationally renowned leadership expert Ken Blanchard, launched an international study to gain insight on the critical skills that make or break a leader. The study concludes that the ability to communicate is the most important characteristic of an effective leader (identified by 43 percent of respondents), and poor communication skills are an ineffective leader's most significant leadership flaw (identified by 41 percent of respondents; Ken Blanchard Companies, 2016). Those who rated communication as an effective leader's most important skill share that leaders who are good communicators have the ability to listen, read body language, provide feedback, and generate effective two-way communication. These communication skills allow them to fully and effectively engage in their work. Conversely, those who identify poor communication skills in their leaders share that their leaders did not communicate at all, over-communicated, communicated through outbursts or anger, or communicated very vaguely (Ken Blanchard Companies, 2016). Most important, poor communicators fail to articulate roles, goals, expectations, and the importance of specific behaviors, which undermines productivity and performance.

Communicating involves many facets. This skill includes the ability to articulate thoughts, listen to others, exchange ideas, read body language, have an awareness of tone, and understand timing. We have identified two essential communication abilities for school leaders interested in transforming their cultures and improving student performance: (1) understanding and confronting relevant data and (2) using persuasion. A leader has to create a compelling, fact-based case for change, and then use his or her ability to convince people to make the organizational challenge their personal challenge.

WHY?

Understanding and Confronting Relevant Data

To help a person understand why he or she should commit to a change, a leader has to provide clear evidence—data—that current practice or policy is not working. Too often, school leaders promote change in practice without providing tangible evidence about why the school needs the change. We have witnessed department and grade-level leaders express that a change is "something the principal wants" when justifying it to their team. Subsequently, the principal says the change came from the central office, the central office identifies state leaders as the source, and state leaders name federal leaders as responsible. A leader who cannot own the change that he or she promotes does not put him- or herself in a good position to expect or demand a staff's commitment.

Leaders who provide tangible evidence exhibit what Stephen R. Covey (1989) calls *principle-centered leadership*. A principle-centered leader focuses people's attention on concrete principles and shared values, and by doing so, the leader empowers everyone who understands those principles to monitor, evaluate, and correct their behavior based on their connection to those principles. Covey (1989) contrasts this with a *personality-centered leader*, who depends on charisma, personal magnetism, and positional power to inspire change and improvement in others, which, in essence, manipulates people, instead of cultivating a real personal commitment. One of the ways principle-centered leaders build commitment to organizational improvement is their constant focus on emphasizing *we* instead of *me* or *I* when engaging in change focus and strategy. This selflessness focuses subordinates on the goals and not the ego or personality of the leader (Bandsuch, Pate, & Thies, 2008). Commitment in a personality-centered environment is unstable and changes as the leader—or leaders'—personality changes. Principle-centered leaders create intrinsic commitment to core organizational values, which leads to a commitment to improvement that goes beyond the current leader's tenure. Developing principle-centered commitment requires a clear understanding of facts, what Jim Collins (2001) calls *confronting the brutal facts*. In studying why some companies make the leap from good to great, Collins (2001) discovers that great companies rise in part because of their willingness to confront the brutal facts (but never lose faith):

> All good-to-great companies begin the process of finding a path to greatness by confronting the brutal facts of their current reality. When you start with an honest and diligent effort to determine the truth of your situation, the right decisions often become self-evident. It is impossible to make good decisions

> without infusing the entire process with an honest confrontation
> of the brutal facts. (p. 88)

Collins (2001) balances his analysis of using brutal facts to stimulate organizational focus and growth with a warning to also never lose faith. He warns that organizations need to use facts in an inspirational context; they can actually use facts counterproductively if the facts lack connections to reasonable goals and a theory of action. Organizations can lose faith if the improvement goals are too high or unreasonable, or if the stark reality is clear, but a plan for improvement is not.

The skill of analyzing data will have great value to a transformational leader who seeks to build a strong commitment to change and a willingness to confront brutal realities. However, keep in mind that exposure to data alone does not always lead to widespread substantive growth. For example, policies like NCLB provided schools with large amounts of data on student academic performance, but the policy did not produce the intended improvement (Guisbond, Neill, & Schaeffer, 2012). An effective leader understands how to use data to create a commitment to goals bigger than the individual and stimulate lasting and powerful intrinsic commitment. Lorna M. Earl and Steven Katz (2006) write about the challenge of using data to motivate change:

> [The challenge is] to follow this engagement [exposure to data]
> with intentional opportunities to develop intrinsic practices in
> order to build the necessary capacities in such a way that they
> become habitual aspects of school work and do not remain at
> the mercy of a policy-bound extrinsic benefactor. (p. 7)

Leaders must use data to drive commitment, not to extend an agenda of coercive compliance. For example, if a school leader can demonstrate to educators that their measurable achievement evidence (data) does not align with the school or district's stated egalitarian commitment to learning for all, he or she could generate a powerful motivating force for change.

As we have shown, the research and evidence support using data to inform leadership practice and stimulate change. Transformational leaders must understand how to properly utilize data so that they can inspire intrinsic commitment to a cause bigger than oneself, identify a starting point for improvement, and stimulate personal ownership and internal agency. Transformational leaders should not, however, use data to scold their followers about past performance like publishing comparative data that would praise one person or school while simultaneously embarrassing another person or school. Data should be used to develop collaborative ownership of a problem and a collective desire to solve that problem.

In the following sections, we present three scenarios designed to help you practice your ability to use data to stimulate intrinsic commitment to change. As you review and reflect on each scenario, we want you to critically analyze your current philosophies and practices. Ask, "Are my current theories and practices aligned or are they incongruent?" and "Does my usage of data make things better or is it making things worse?" Consider the research and evidence presented in this chapter to guide your answers and responses. After each scenario, we provide some important considerations designed to help you reflect on your own thinking and habits as they relate to the research and the aim of each scenario.

SCENARIO ONE: *Dealing With a Pessimistic View of Data*

You are a new principal assuming leadership at an elementary school that has had three different principals in the previous five years. The previous principal served for two years, and during that time, school performance on state mathematics and reading tests dropped. The teaching staff are a mix of 40 percent veteran teachers (with more than ten years of teaching experience) and 60 percent teachers who are new to the school and the profession (with less than five years of teaching experience). The previous principal had a very authoritarian style. He spent a lot of time collecting data from classroom walkthroughs and giving negative feedback to teachers about their performance. Consequently, teachers developed a pessimistic view of data. The staff started to view data as a tool for criticism and for leadership to assert authority, rather than as a tool for growth and development.

You begin your tenure with a review of past performance. The data make it evident that the school has a huge deficit in literacy (a brutal fact). You have a literacy background, including a bachelor's and a master's degree in literacy education. In fact, you spent three years as a literacy coach and had a very strong track record in increasing literacy. So how would you, as the new principal, effectively use data to confront the necessity to improve literacy practices—especially considering that a principal used data as a tool to put down teachers in the past? Use figure 2.1 to reflect on this scenario and brainstorm strategies.

Scenario One: Dealing With a Pessimistic View of Data	Strategies
What data would you gather?	• • •
How would you present the data to appeal to a sense of commitment?	• • •
How would you use the facts to inform, not to scold?	• • •
How would you use the facts to stimulate personal ownership and internal agency?	• • •

Figure 2.1: Strategies for dealing with a pessimistic view of data.

*Visit **go.SolutionTree.com/leadership** for a free reproducible version of this figure.*

Consider the following when reflecting on this scenario.

▸ Remember the goal of utilizing data—to build awareness around an important need (brutal fact).

▸ The focus is cognitive (logical), not emotional. Your goal is not to build relationships (we cover this in chapter 3, page 43); it is to build a sense of urgency and ownership around a set of uncomfortable facts.

▸ Consider if you use facts to push a personal agenda and not to solicit feedback and develop collective responsibility. If you do, how has that habit affected collective responsibility for change?

 SCENARIO TWO: *Improving On What Is Already Considered Great*

The board of education has declared that every school in your district must produce a comprehensive school-improvement plan within sixty days. The plan requires that each school create at least five school-improvement goals; analyze student state test results in mathematics, reading, and science; and disaggregate those results by race, gender, socioeconomic status, disability, home language, and

WHY?

student mobility. The plan also requires each school to analyze student engagement data like attendance, behavioral violations, failure rate, and rate of enrollment in advanced courses. Finally, the board requires each school to analyze opinion survey results from students, parents, and community members.

You are the principal at an award-winning middle school in this district. State test results from the previous year placed your school in the top 5 percent of student proficiency in mathematics and reading and in the top 20 percent in science. You lead a veteran teaching staff where more than 85 percent of the teaching staff have more than ten years of experience, and 75 percent of those teachers have only taught in your school. You have served as this school's principal for fourteen years, so you have established strong personal relationships with staff members. You afford them a tremendous amount of professional autonomy. People inside and outside the school thrive on the narrative that this school is great; in fact, most describe it as utopian.

As you analyze the data from the board of education, you find data that contradict some prevailing assumptions about your school. Students with disabilities failed the state science test at a rate of 55 percent, compared with the school average of 11 percent. Latino students, who make up 8 percent of the school population, receive 78 percent of student disciplinary suspensions. Twelve percent of students live in economically disadvantaged homes, but an analysis of advanced course enrollment reveals that no economically disadvantaged students are enrolled in the school's most challenging courses. The school appears utopian, but as you examine very specific performance data, you discover that the utopian experience does not apply equally to all students. How would you engage your staff in a discussion of the facts that stimulates an intrinsic need to improve? Use figure 2.2 to reflect on this scenario and brainstorm strategies.

Consider the following when reflecting on this scenario.

▸ Are equity and fairness important to you? If so, do you regularly measure equity and present the brutal facts to your staff? If not, what drives you to disregard it or overlook it?

▸ Do you have a fear of exposing less-than-flattering realities to your subordinates? Do you fear a negative response? Do you fear that they will not be receptive?

▸ Is it better to own the performance data school district leadership has provided, or is it better to question the validity of the inquiry and vilify the school district leadership? Which would lead to intrinsic ownership and commitment?

Scenario Two: Improving On What Is Already Considered Great	Strategies
What data would you gather?	• • •
How would you present the data to appeal to a sense of commitment?	• • •
How would you use the facts to inform, not to scold?	• • •
How would you use the facts to stimulate personal ownership and internal agency?	• • •

Figure 2.2: Strategies for improving on what is already considered great.

Visit go.SolutionTree.com/leadership for a free reproducible version of this figure.

SCENARIO THREE: *Facing Conflict, Lack of Direction, and Power Struggles*

You are the new superintendent of a large city school district. The district has slightly over one hundred thousand enrolled students. The district is operating on a budget deficit, and students' state test scores in mathematics and reading rank in the bottom 25 percent in the state. Student graduation rates hover around 60 percent, but high school graduation data are skewed because the rate only applies to students who enter their senior year and complete it by the end of that academic year. The data do not take into consideration students who never make it to their senior year. District climate surveys reveal less than 5 percent of district employees feel that the district is moving in the right direction and that district leadership has an effective improvement plan.

You have inherited a school district that has a history of implementing system-wide reform without properly vetting the process, building systemwide consensus, or creating the infrastructure to properly implement the reform. Employees describe the district as a "laboratory rat" that anyone with a slick idea, the right sales pitch, and the proper political influence can engage in a clinical study. The previous superintendent was indicted on charges of corruption and accepting a bribe from a consulting firm that received a no-bid contract for the last systemwide initiative.

Your analysis of your new district's reality shows that conflict, lack of direction, and power struggles are the norm. The most disturbing piece of data that you analyze reveals that the district turns over 60 percent of its school principals and 40 percent of its teaching staff every year. In your previous work assignment, you worked in a school district that implemented a long-term plan focused on student literacy, equity, and high school graduation; had a high employee retention rate; and cultivated talent internally to ensure long-term success. You want to convince your new district's school board, district and school leaders, teachers, and community that they must prioritize and invest in employee recruitment, training, and retention if they hope to achieve long-term success. How would you use data to build commitment to your vision and direction for the school district? Use figure 2.3 to reflect on this scenario and brainstorm strategies.

Scenario Three: Facing Conflict, Lack of Direction, and Power Struggles	Strategies
What data would you gather?	• • •
How would you present the data to appeal to a sense of commitment?	• • •
How would you use the facts to inform, not to scold?	• • •
How would you use the facts to stimulate personal ownership and internal agency?	• • •

Figure 2.3: Strategies for facing conflict, lack of direction, and power struggles.

*Visit **go.SolutionTree.com/leadership** for a free reproducible version of this figure.*

Consider the following when reflecting on this scenario.

- ▶ Considering that your goal is a long-term commitment to change, how would you separate issues of great importance from those with minor importance?

- ▶ Given the history of this school district, how modest should your goals be? Would being too ambitious too soon undermine faith in improvement and intrinsic commitment?

- ▶ Consider being the chief communicator of district direction and priorities and not delegating to subordinates given the system's history of distrust and corruption.

WHY?

A leader's effective use of data can help staff understand why some realities need to change and why some needs are more important than others. Facts create an environment that makes change logical. For the next phase in transforming a culture, a leader must have the ability to argue for a specific change in practice that everyone agrees benefits the whole. Data can help people understand why they need to change, but they need more than data to convince them that the leader's vision is the right way to engage in the change.

Using Persuasion

Leadership is an exercise in influence, and a very powerful component of influence is the ability to help other people see and embrace your vision with the same level of clarity you have achieved. Transformational leaders understand how to use the power of persuasion. Persuasive communication utilizes written or spoken communication that conveys information, thoughts, emotions, logic, and arguments in a way that influences a person's perception about a thing or an event (Boundless, 2013). Persuasive communication has five goals.

1. **To stimulate:** Recognize a problem and the collective need to solve it.

2. **To convince:** Create consensus around a specific proposal for change.

3. **To call to action:** Desire to accept the inconvenience of change in exchange for the promise of improvement.

4. **To increase consideration:** Intellectually engage all stakeholders in the process of finding a common solution.

5. **To promote tolerance of alternative perspectives:** Emphasize *we* over *me*.

As consultants, we travel the world and attempt to convince educators that the theories, strategies, and practices we promote are in their best interest and have a high likelihood of positively impacting their environment. We utilize both written and verbal forms of communication to build this commitment to and optimism about our ideas. A transformational leader has to develop this capacity as part of his or her leadership toolbox.

One important factor of communicating persuasively is context. Leaders need to communicate how an idea, strategy, or practice has helped others in similar situations. In other words, they need to answer, "How has this concept worked in schools like ours?" for staff. We believe this question is logical and an essential part of stimulating intrinsic commitment. Looking to the research gives leaders one way to answer this question.

In her book *Inside Teaching: How Classroom Life Undermines Reform*, Mary M. Kennedy (2005) asserts that leaders have abused the phrase *the research says*. She argues that leaders tend to use research conclusions that they don't understand, generalizing the findings to teachers in a way that criticizes their current practice in a frail attempt to shame them into trying something different (Kennedy, 2005). Kennedy (2005) goes on to claim that if leaders better understood research and became better research consumers, they could skillfully connect teachers with practices that would match their daily contexts, increasing the likelihood that they would embrace those strategies. Just because the research *says* something works doesn't mean that it works in every context.

Another critical factor of persuasive communication is the ability to argue without becoming argumentative. In other words, a transformational leader has to anticipate resistance to his or her idea and prepare to answer critiques before initiating the communication and without alienating the person who disagrees. Cynicism results when people have years of exposure to negative stimulation about a particular topic or structure without it causing any tangible growth or improvement. An effective leader understands the organizational culture and proactively tries to create a new narrative before simply diving in to change a negative environment (Gumperz & Cook-Gumperz, 2008). When considering delivering a pitch for change, it helps to play the proverbial devil's advocate and prepare meaningful and factual responses to ideas and assumptions that clash with one's optimistic vision for the future.

Finally, persuasion requires attention to detail. Before people can feel comfortable with changing their behaviors, they want to know exactly how this change will work and how it will affect their norms and routines. In her *Inc.* magazine article about the late Apple cofounder and CEO Steve Jobs's legacy, Geil Browning (2013) notes Jobs's attention to detail. She credits it as a major reason for his success at transforming Apple and the entire world of personal computing. Browning (2013) declares that Jobs was a *structured thinker*; a structured thinker approaches details in the following manner.

- ▸ **Learn by doing:** Provide plenty of how-to information, and do not deviate from the goal or target.

- ▸ **Want practicality:** Make communication convey common-sense rationale in straightforward terms.

- ▸ **Work sequentially:** Hand out a step-by-step implementation plan and a guide for how things need to be done.

- ▸ **Provide guidelines:** Communicate in concrete terms and explain the rules because ideas are great, but freewheeling, nebulous concepts are not.

The ability to sell an idea conceptually will excite people in the present. But if a leader cannot structure the idea in a practical way, it will disappoint people in the future when they find that they lack necessary details for successful implementation.

In order to persuade people to embrace an idea that inspires intrinsic commitment to change, transformational leaders must understand how to communicate context, what to expect in terms of resistance, and how to communicate details. In the following sections, we present three scenarios designed to help you practice your ability to use persuasion to stimulate intrinsic commitment to change. As you review and reflect on each scenario, we want you to critically analyze your current philosophies and practices. Ask, "Are my current theories and practices aligned or are they incongruent?" "Does my usage of persuasion make things better or is it making things worse?" Consider the research and evidence presented in this chapter to guide your answers and responses. After each scenario, we provide some important considerations designed to help you reflect on your own thinking and habits as they relate to the research and the aim of each scenario.

WHY?

SCENARIO ONE: *Seeing the Errors in Current Practice*

You're a high school counselor in your second year of practice at your current school, though you have been an educator for fifteen years. You are concerned about the number of students receiving out-of-school suspension for minor disciplinary infractions. As a counselor, you get a bird's-eye view of the impact that days away from school have on students' grades, credit acquisition, and, ultimately, graduation rate. You review the school data on student disciplinary infractions and find that nearly 80 percent of the students receiving suspensions of three days or less receive them for three primary violations: (1) insubordination, (2) classroom disruption, and (3) failure to follow school rules. As a counselor, you do not have the authority to enforce a change in policy, but you have the opportunity to persuade teachers and administrators in your school to change the way they issue suspension as a disciplinary measure.

Before accepting employment in your current school, you served as a teacher in a high school that embraced the restorative justice theory (Anfara, Evans, & Lester, 2013). Instead of punishing students, your former school created an environment and structures that helped students recognize the error of their ways and provided opportunities for students to commit acts of service that atoned for their misdeeds and added value to the school culture. This method resulted in a 90 percent reduction in student infractions, and it nearly eliminated out-of-school suspensions. You and your former colleagues received intensive professional development in restorative justice methods, and you even had an opportunity to share your success with others at a national conference.

You recognize that the current situation at your high school mirrors that of your former school, and you believe restorative justice would perfectly respond to the high rate of disciplinary infractions. In the short time that you have served in your position, you have observed that both administrators and teachers passionately enforce strict student behavior policies and administer punishment for students who do not adhere to those policies. Your observation and school data reveal that this mindset and method have had no impact on student behavior; they have only led to a culture of conflict and student alienation. The experience and insight that you gained at your former school make it difficult for you to passively dissociate yourself from this reality. How would you use the power of persuasion to convince your colleagues to consider the errors of their current practice and embrace restorative justice in the same way that you do? Use figure 2.4 to reflect on this scenario and brainstorm strategies.

Scenario One: Seeing the Errors in Current Practice	Strategies
How would you help people recognize the importance of your idea in their context and reality?	• • •
What resistance or arguments might you expect the people you are trying to influence to pose so they can devalue your proposal?	• • •
How would you counter their arguments?	• • •
What details or concrete processes would you share to increase the confidence of those you are trying to influence?	• • •

Figure 2.4: Strategies for seeing the errors in current practice.

Visit **go.SolutionTree.com/leadership** *for a free reproducible version of this figure.*

Consider the following when reflecting on this scenario.

▶ Narratives, examples, and stories have a positive influence on shaping thinking. Consider sharing stories of success, not just data, with this new staff to make the idea more vivid and demystify the process.

▶ Consider sharing some pitfalls and some challenges that you experienced at your old school when implementing this practice and sharing how you and your colleagues resolved those issues.

▶ Do not be afraid to challenge the ineffectiveness of the old punitive model; make them defend the old model as vigorously as they try to make you defend your proposal.

SCENARIO TWO: *Selling an Initiative to Content Stakeholders*

You are a middle school principal who truly embraces the idea of egalitarianism. You actually believe what the school mission states when it claims that your fundamental purpose as an institution is to ensure learning and success for all students. By all accounts, your school is beloved by those who work there, and school indicators of success reveal that your school has a high rating compared with other schools in your state and school district. As you review your performance data, you discover that only 15 percent of your students are enrolled in accelerated mathematics and reading courses. In fact, your school's master schedule restricts student access by design by only offering two sections of accelerated mathematics and reading courses by grade level. Finally, parents of the 15 percent of students enrolled in accelerated courses are your most involved and politically active parents, and they covet the exclusive nature of their child's placement in these limited courses. You find this reality unsettling.

You attend a national conference and learn of a school that has created a system that automatically places all students into accelerated academic courses. You arrange a visit to this school and witness its multitiered support system that differentiates student support based on need. Students are experiencing tremendous academic growth, and the school has performance data to validate the success of its system. This thoroughly impresses you, and you resolve to create a similar system at your school.

As you return from your visit, your stomach starts to churn. Images of angry parents, phone calls from school board members, and indifferent stares from comfortable staff members flash through your mind. How would you persuade a group of content people that they need to be inconvenienced and work hard through painful substantive change to raise student achievement to unprecedented heights? Use figure 2.5 to reflect on this scenario and brainstorm strategies.

Consider the following when reflecting on this scenario.

▶ Consider your allies within the school and among district leadership. Are there others who believe your school can improve? What support could they provide professionally and politically?

▶ Consider balancing the general narrative from a culture of exclusive praise to one that considers ways to get better and confronting brutal facts on a more regular basis. People are less prone to change if they are satisfied with their current reality.

▶ Put together a team of diverse staff members (administrators, counselors, teachers, and district office staff) to oversee the implementation process. Doubts and uncertainty breed fear. The more organized and seamless the transition, the higher the likelihood of universal implementation.

Scenario Two: Selling an Initiative to Content Stakeholders	Strategies
How would you help people recognize the importance of your idea in their context and reality?	• • •
What resistance or arguments might you expect the people you are trying to influence to pose so they can devalue your proposal?	• • •
How would you counter their arguments?	• • •
What details or concrete processes would you share to increase the confidence of those you are trying to influence?	• • •

Figure 2.5: Strategies for selling an initiative to content stakeholders.

Visit **go.SolutionTree.com/leadership** *for a free reproducible version of this figure.*

SCENARIO THREE: *Convincing a Large Group of Teachers*

You are a K–12 school district's director of instruction. You supervise the practice of nearly one thousand teachers, and you have influence over curriculum, instruction, assessment, and instructional resources. During the recent district leadership data retreat, you revealed to your administrative colleagues that close to 40 percent of secondary school students received a failing grade in at least one academic course (mathematics, reading, social studies, or science) during the previous school year. As you analyzed this trend chronologically, you shared that this statistical reality has existed for at least the previous seven years. You expressed to your administrative colleagues that you want to reduce the frequency of failing grades by 50 percent for the upcoming school year. Your investigation also revealed that 90 percent of report cards that listed a failing grade indicated "classwork not completed" and "poor participation" in the comments section.

You ascended to your current supervisory position in part because of your penchant for educational research, particularly research on assessment. As a teacher, you utilized a standards-based grading technique and reported student progress based on growth in competence in mastering your course's learning objectives.

WHY?

You skillfully provided feedback, and you gave students multiple opportunities to demonstrate mastery. This created an environment where almost no students failed.

How would you persuade nearly one thousand teachers to examine the effect of failing student grades and consider standards-based grading as an alternative to their current practice, which has obviously not positively impacted the district's rate of course passing? Use figure 2.6 to reflect on this scenario and brainstorm strategies.

Scenario Three: Convincing a Large Group of Teachers	Strategies
How would you help people recognize the importance of your idea in their context and reality?	• • •
What resistance or arguments might you expect the people you are trying to influence to pose so they can devalue your proposal?	• • •
How would you counter their arguments?	• • •
What details or concrete processes would you share to increase the confidence of those you are trying to influence?	• • •

Figure 2.6: Strategies for convincing a large group of teachers.

*Visit **go.SolutionTree.com/leadership** for a free reproducible version of this figure.*

Consider the following when reflecting on this scenario.

▸ Remember that the teachers' apprehension about change is not directed at you personally. Teachers collectively lack an understanding of better assessment practice. The practice, not the person, needs improvement.

▸ What made you excited about standards-based grading, and what insight helped shift your paradigm? If it helped shape your thinking, there is a high likelihood that it will have a similar effect on a lot of teachers you supervise.

▶ Consider choosing a few pilot schools to test your theory. Systemic change is very difficult, and providing evidence of effectiveness at a few schools might make the case stronger when scaling the practice at a district level.

Conclusion

Leaders who want to build consensus must create a cognitive and philosophical connection with their followers, which makes communication an invaluable skill. People will likely resist change if they don't clearly understand why they need to change. Too often, leaders assume that their subordinates understand what they are thinking and that they have all the tools, information, and exposure necessary to embrace the vision for change. Unless educators develop the ability to read minds, school and district leaders have to clearly and positively communicate their rationale with data, use context to persuade and intrinsically motivate people, and anticipate resistance and positively respond to it. Use the rating scale in figure 2.7 to rate your proficiency in communicating the rationale in each of the skill areas.

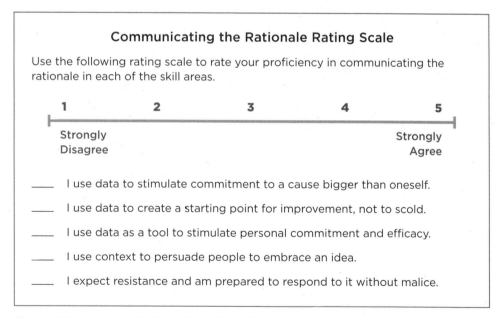

Figure 2.7: Communicating the rationale rating scale.

*Visit **go.SolutionTree.com/leadership** for a free reproducible version of this figure.*

3

Establishing Trust:
Making an Emotional Investment

A first-time principal nervously prepares for her first formal encounter with her new faculty. All principals remember this important moment in their school leadership journey. She envisions looking at the smiling faces of her new colleagues with an anticipation that they will welcome her into their school with open arms.

A change of venue is scary under almost any circumstance, but walking into a new environment to find unfriendly, cold stares would be any new principal's worst nightmare. She is the school's third principal in the previous three years. Each of the previous principals' tenures ended in scandal and conflict. She has inherited that legacy.

As the principal, full of ideas, vision, and optimism, walks into the faculty meeting, she confronts a sea of frowns and negative body language. Unless she makes an emotional connection and breaks the ice with her new colleagues, they are probably not likely to hear and consider, let alone implement, her vision for school change. Unfortunately, because of the instability and lack of longevity at the school-leadership level, the principal's situation is all too common.

Creating a rational connection to organizational purpose and direction—the need to understand *why* change is necessary—is important, but leaders must couple such enlightenment with trust. Good leaders know how to connect people to purpose, but transformational leaders also understand that people have to connect with other people—the *who*. David L. Mineo (2014) writes, "Trust is the glue that binds the leader to her/his followers and provides the capacity for organizational and leadership success" (p. 1). Organizational transformation becomes very difficult when the followers do not trust the person or people leading them.

Trust is much more abstract than communication. It relies on individual experiences, involves emotion, and can evolve differently from person to person. What one person requires to establish trust may differ greatly from what another person requires. For example, a third-year teacher who has only practiced under one principal's tutelage may view trust very differently than a veteran teacher of twenty years who has served under seven principals with very different leadership styles. A new leader has to survey the environment and assess the trust level before pushing people into change at an accelerated pace. Jim Dougherty (2013), a former CEO and business professor, writes:

> Establishing trust is *the* top priority. Whether you are taking over a small department, an entire division, a company, or even a Boy Scout troop, the first thing you must get is the trust of the members of that entity. When asked, most leaders will agree to this notion, but few do anything to act on it.

The inability to acknowledge and act on a trust gap can have devastating consequences on a leader's effectiveness.

Establishing Trust as a Leadership Skill

In one survey of employees at 450 companies, 69 percent of respondents agreed with the statement, "I just don't know who to trust anymore" (Hurley, 2006). When leadership loses trust, followers start to disconnect from the leader's guidance, direction, and authority and eventually from the entire organization (Evans, 1996). Roger J. Givens (2008) finds that trust in leadership has the greatest correlation to worker self-efficacy, and leadership trust could be the difference between organizational success or failure. Because schools are so essential to a society's well-being, they have even higher stakes. When educators, especially teachers, lose faith in the organization and its purpose, it can have real negative consequences on students.

The School Leaders Network (2014) finds that principals account for 25 percent of a school's total influence on improving student academic performance; however, it also finds that it can take a new principal up to three years to positively influence mathematics and reading achievement and at least five years to fully implement a vision for improvement. In reality, less than 50 percent of new principals make it past three years of service, and only 30 percent last beyond five years. When analyzing the causes of principal turnover and strategizing to increase retention, the School Leaders Network (2014) finds that the first, most crucial factor for increasing retention is creating "strong trusting relationships with peers" (p. 16). Trust matters, and building trust involves more than possessing an endearing personality and being liked by others.

Trustworthiness (reliability) and *likability* (an affable nature) are very different things. A person can like someone he or she distrusts and trust someone he or she dislikes. We are not arguing that being affable and personable are bad traits. In fact, we would recommend that leaders display traits of likability as often as possible. But, ultimately, trustworthiness is much more important than likability when it comes to stimulating commitment to change behavior. A series of studies conducted in the 1980s and 1990s on celebrity product endorsement supports this conclusion. Picking the right spokesperson for a product can either make or break the success of a product or service. Prior to this emerging body of research, most companies picked spokespeople on a hunch rather than based on concrete scientific predictors. The most important element in effective product endorsement, however, is trustworthiness at almost double the impact of charisma and likability (Miciak & Shanklin, 1994).

When a leader displays a need for social approval, and that need clashes with the courage necessary to improve organizational performance and challenge professional practice, it actually diminishes that leader's credibility (Alicke et al., 1992). For example, in our work in schools, we often witness school principals and superintendents make the mistake of joking about unprofessional behavior, presumably to boost their likability among their subordinates. For instance, during professional development sessions held in large auditoriums, teachers commonly fill the seats from the back to the front, often leaving rows of empty seats between the presenter and the stage. These professional development sessions typically begin with an opening statement and introduction by a school or district administrator. It is not uncommon for these leaders to begin their introduction by making jokes about their staff members' seating choices, such as, "Everyone is sitting in the back, just like at church!" These type of comments generally inspire a chuckle from the audience, but they don't inspire respect for the leader or professional norms. Rather, they reinforce negative stereotypes about low organizational expectations. The leaders' attempt to validate the teachers' unprofessional seating arrangement with humor subtly implies that the teachers are not interested in the training or gives permission to not take it seriously. This type of behavior only serves to define the leaders as insincere and people pleasers, not reliable examples of high character.

Building trust is much more substantive than appearing likable, and according to Covey (2009), it includes two dimensions: (1) character and (2) competence.

WHO?

He states, "Character includes your integrity, motive, and intent with people. Competence includes your capabilities, skills, results, and track record. Both dimensions are vital" (Covey, 2009). Transformational leaders can establish greater influence by developing these two dimensions. Leaders can prove their good character by understanding the context and challenges of those they lead (developing empathy). They can prove their competence through displays of skill, good judgment, knowledge, and wisdom that produce a climate for change and success (establishing credibility).

Character: Developing Empathy

Leaders often find it challenging to understand exactly what it means to develop empathy. Empathy is not synonymous with sympathy. Colleen Kettenhofen (n.d.) describes the difference in the following manner:

> To discover what empathy is, let's first talk about what it is not. Empathy is not sympathy. It does not mean you have to agree with how someone is feeling, or even relate to their feelings. Instead, empathy is all about the awareness of other people's feelings—even when you can't sympathize with them!

Empathy does not require a leader to experience the same emotion another person experiences; it requires that he or she understand the emotion and consider it when leading.

Far too often, schools thrust leaders into their leadership position and pressure them to immediately improve measurable indicators of school success. Leaders find it hard to develop empathy for others when their supervisors expect immediate results. The pressure to immediately improve school performance is one reason that principals do not make it beyond five years of service (Stolp, 1994). The turnover rate is especially high at schools identified for school improvement by state authorities. The principal turnover rate at these schools is more than double the rate of schools not identified for mandated improvement (Grissom & Bartanen, 2018). The emotional disconnect also adversely affects teachers, who leave the profession in large numbers and report increased absenteeism in high-pressure, low-support environments (Keller, 2008). Schools, especially schools that face pressure to improve, can produce high-stress environments. Leaders who do not understand stress and the impact it has on school employees are doomed to fail, even if they have a brilliant vision for improvement. Stressed-out people do not respond to leaders who lack empathy (Tavakoli, 2010).

Michael Fullan (2011) points out that focusing on improvement and developing empathy are not mutually exclusive. He writes that effective change leaders should remember two things:

> (1) When you are on a crucial mission, stay the course against all odds; and (2) be impressively empathetic when it comes to opposition in the early stages. . . . Leaders in sustained successful organizations focus on a small number of core priorities, stay on message, and develop others toward the same end, making corrections as new learning occurs. (Fullan, 2011, p. 30)

An effective leader focuses on improving organizational performance, but at the same time, he or she realizes that all the organization's members must possess a personal passion to improve organizational performance. Empathy becomes important for a transformational leader as he or she recognizes that some followers have experienced emotional trauma, and that the unproductive attitudes and dispositions they may display are situational and can adjust. Empathy is a tool for adjusting attitude; it can turn an adversary into an advocate. We break down empathy into three specific skills: (1) displaying genuine concern, (2) listening without rebuttal, and (3) collaborating to move forward.

Simon Sinek, an internationally celebrated expert on effective leadership, perfectly articulates the skill of displaying genuine concern. Sinek writes, "Empathy—the ability to recognize and share other people's feelings—is the most important instrument in a leader's toolbox. . . . It can be expressed in the simple words, 'Is everything OK?'" (as cited in Levitt, 2017). In order to truly display concern, a leader has to learn how to listen to understand, not listen to inform. People experiencing emotional discomfort are not concerned about another person's opinion of their pain or their pain's legitimacy; they simply want someone to understand. Conversations become hostile when a listener deceives a speaker by responding with disingenuous concern followed by unsolicited advice. Not only does it ruin a potentially powerful and unifying moment, but it produces a wedge between the parties that could last for years (Patterson, Grenny, McMillan, & Switzler, 2002). By listening, validating, and exhibiting genuine concern about the well-being of those under his or her care and direction, a leader is repairing damage that interferes with organizational progress. The healing is for a purpose, to improve the contribution of a vital team member. Empathy has to eventually lead to a resolution. The goal of this skill is not to turn a leader into a pseudo-therapist. If, as Sinek describes, a leader can show genuine concern with the question, "Is everything OK?" then the leader can find a collaborative resolution by simply asking, "How do we move

WHO?

forward?" The emotional trauma was a barrier that needed to be removed so that the subordinate could focus his or her efforts on organizational goals and objectives, not on the unresolved emotional issues.

In the following sections, we present three scenarios designed to help you practice your ability to use data to stimulate intrinsic commitment to change. As you review and reflect on each scenario, we want you to critically analyze your current philosophies and practices. Ask, "Are my current theories and practices aligned or are they incongruent?" "Do I establish trust with those I lead?" Consider the research and evidence presented in this chapter to guide your answers and responses. After each scenario, we provide some important considerations designed to help you reflect on your own thinking and habits as they relate to the research and the aim of each scenario.

SCENARIO ONE: *Understanding the Challenges of Change*

You are the principal at a high-performing elementary school. Your school has won several awards for student academic achievement, including your state's highest honor, the Blue Ribbon award. The state department of education just notified you that the previous year's state academic testing results reveal that the economically disadvantaged students at your school performed significantly lower than the other students, and the gap is so large that the state has placed your school in the *needs improvement* category.

This achievement disparity among students based on socioeconomic status has upset you personally for three years. You attempted to inspire your staff to enthusiastically take on the challenge of improving student performance in the past; you exposed them to data and cited research, but that approach did not stimulate the response you wanted. In addition, the data revealed that most economically disadvantaged students in the school are also very mobile. On average, an economically disadvantaged student stays in your school for seven months. So when the staff start to see signs of progress with these students, most of them move on to other schools.

Staff members in your school pride themselves on being hardworking student advocates. Most performance indicators would validate that belief, but the data concerning economically disadvantaged students disrupt that narrative, making it a difficult discussion topic. In the past, you could put the finding aside, but now, because of the state's declaration, you have to confront this anomaly in your data. Your staff have traditionally coped with this issue by blaming the students and the circumstances that created this crisis. You regularly hear, "I can't be their teacher and their parent!" or "If they wouldn't move so much, we could help them!" or "If I concentrate on their needs, it will take time and resources from my good students, and that isn't fair!" Personally, you have observed that, at best, the staff have half-heartedly attempted to support economically disadvantaged and mobile students in the past, and the school's intervention methods and systems could greatly improve.

How would you engage staff members in talking about this disparity with empathy, while also helping them understand that their practices and efforts can improve? Use figure 3.1 to reflect on this scenario and brainstorm strategies.

Scenario One: Understanding the Challenges of Change	Strategies
How would you create opportunities to demonstrate genuine concern about the emotions of those you lead?	• • •
What types of strategies would you use to stay fully engaged, process concerns, and refrain from giving personal opinions or rebuttals?	• • •
How would you collaborate with those you lead to create a collaborative resolution to their stated issues?	• • •
How would you continue to demonstrate empathy throughout the entire change process?	• • •

Figure 3.1: Strategies for understanding the challenges of change.

*Visit **go.SolutionTree.com/leadership** for a free reproducible version of this figure.*

Consider the following when reflecting on this scenario.

▸ Be careful not to mix your own personal feelings about equity and egalitarianism when assessing the emotional needs of this staff.

▸ Remember that their need is emotional, not rational; data (brutal facts) will not inspire them. Doubling down on facts and evidence will make the emotional wound worse.

WHO?

▶ You want to hear their frustrations and concerns to soothe their anxieties, but you ultimately have to pivot to resolutions. You are not a therapist.

SCENARIO TWO: *Justifying a High-Budget Program*

You are a superintendent in a small, rural school district. Because of recent economic hardships, property values in your community have decreased significantly, and the tax revenue collected for school funding will decrease by 20 percent. This shock to the school district budget has necessitated emergency budget cuts, including cutting ten teaching jobs and increasing class sizes from twenty-eight students to thirty-eight students. Staff received notification of the changes during the summer. Now that teachers have returned to school, it is apparent that the changes have greatly affected morale.

The budget cuts could not have come at a worse time. You have forged a year-long relationship with a consulting firm to train your teachers in a new reading program, and this arrangement was established before the emergency budget cuts. The consulting firm contract totals $1.4 million. This training, and all the support materials, are paid for through federal funds, which the decreasing tax revenue will not affect. Additionally, the federal funds have strict stipulations about how they can be spent, and general employee salaries and class-size reduction are forbidden expenditures. However, people within the school district and the community begin to talk about the high cost of the reading initiative. You hear whispers that you and the board of education are involved in corruption and that you will personally benefit from the relationship with the consulting firm.

As a former reading teacher, you firmly believe that the new reading program will greatly impact student reading proficiency. Your school district's student reading proficiency ranks in the bottom 10 percent among all districts in your state. This reality has persisted for over twenty years. In fact, the board of education hired you because of your reading expertise and gave you the green light to move forward with the expensive reading initiative as a means to address this achievement issue. How would you use empathy to inspire the teachers, school administrators, and community members with the same level of enthusiasm for the reading program that you possess? Use figure 3.2 to reflect on this scenario and brainstorm strategies.

Scenario Two: Justifying a High-Budget Program	Strategies
How would you create opportunities to demonstrate genuine concern about the emotions of those you lead?	• • •
What types of strategies would you use to stay fully engaged, process concerns, and refrain from giving personal opinions or rebuttals?	• • •
How would you collaborate with those you lead to create a collaborative resolution to their stated issues?	• • •
How would you continue to demonstrate empathy throughout the entire change process?	• • •

Figure 3.2: Strategies for justifying a high-budget program.

*Visit **go.SolutionTree.com/leadership** for a free reproducible version of this figure.*

Consider the following when reflecting on this scenario.

▶ This is a small school district and the job losses represent close friendships and long relationships. To many of the remaining employees, the cuts are not about dollars and cents; they are about lost relationships and the human impact.

▶ You have a knowledge of school funding and law that the average community member and school employee may not possess. Decisions that seem simple and logical to you may not seem as logical to those who do not possess the knowledge of law and school finance that you hold.

▶ Don't overreact to strong displeasure voiced about the decisions made. The anger is about the impact of the decisions you made, not about you personally. Sincerely listening to the impact of those decisions is important in the emotional healing process.

WHO?

SCENARIO THREE: *Calming Fears*

You are a new high school principal. Your high school is located in a city that has experienced deindustrialization. It has a very high unemployment rate, and the population has rapidly declined, which, in turn, has led to lower student enrollment and a sharp decline in financial resources. Your school has a student capacity of fifteen hundred, but current enrollment is only six hundred. The school, which utilizes only two of the building's four stories, has a lot of empty space.

The community around the school has experienced a lot of gang violence. The general consensus is that the neighborhood is dangerous. The school allocates the largest amount of its budget for security; in fact, the school employs more security officers than mathematics and science teachers. All the school's entrances have metal detectors, and all students and visitors must be screened before entering. The data show that the district has not experienced a school shooting or an assault with a weapon in twenty years, and security officers have never confiscated a knife or gun from a student since the school began using metal detectors and its current security protocol.

You feel most troubled about poor student achievement, not school security. The school has an annual graduation rate of only 55 percent. You attended a similar school as a young student, and you can remember the personal shame you felt each day as you walked through metal detectors at your school's entrance and had your belongings searched by school security officers. It made you feel like a criminal even though you had broken no laws. You believe an overemphasis on security spending when the data do not validate such an investment perpetuates the school's low achievement and graduation rate. You want to reallocate 50 percent of the school's security budget to academic support resources. How would you demonstrate empathy for the staff's fears, while simultaneously gaining support to reallocate security resources toward academic support resources? Use figure 3.3 to reflect on this scenario and brainstorm strategies.

Consider the following when reflecting on this scenario.

▶ Your personal experience as a student has shaped your view of school security and its impact on school culture. When addressing your staff's emotional needs, remember that your experience may not be the norm for many of your teachers and staff members.

▶ Before articulating your desire to boost student academic support, validate the safety fears that some of the staff members possess. In essence, what is your plan for keeping the campus safe while also

Scenario Three: Calming Fears	Strategies
How would you create opportunities to demonstrate genuine concern about the emotions of those you lead?	• • •
What types of strategies would you use to stay fully engaged, process concerns, and refrain from giving personal opinions or rebuttals?	• • •
How would you collaborate with those you lead to create a collaborative resolution to their stated issues?	• • •
How would you continue to demonstrate empathy throughout the entire change process?	• • •

Figure 3.3: Strategies for calming fears.

*Visit **go.SolutionTree.com/leadership** for a free reproducible version of this figure.*

addressing student academic needs? The staff do not want to hear "safety *or* achievement." They want to hear "safety *and* achievement."

▸ You might want to consider monitoring a key set of data around safety (such as assaults, theft, and weapons violations) after reducing security resources to provide the staff with some evidence of the impact of the security changes. If you can prove that the reduction of security resources has not led to a significant safety risk, it should increase the staff's confidence in you as a decision maker.

The skill of trust is about building a personal bond with those that you lead. Empathy is a very powerful tool that reinforces a leader's humanity. It demonstrates that the leader cares about people and is genuinely concerned about their well-being. Though important, this is only one side of the trust equation. The other side is not quite as tender; it's establishing credibility. If a person's decision to change behavior hinges on his or her trust in leadership, he or she has to acknowledge more than just a leader's humanity; he or she needs to witness competence.

WHO?

Competence: Establishing Credibility

Credibility is not easy to establish, but once in place, it acts as a very powerful influencer. Consider, for example, a child who is learning to swim. He or she recognizes that there is danger and will not jump into the water without a trusted instructor or parent (or other caregiver) present. The child is willing to take a risk and jump into deep water knowing that his or her instructor or parent will keep him or her from harm's way. If a leader wants those he or she leads to jump into change without reservation, he or she must first establish credibility. Peter Economy (2015) writes, "Trust goes hand in hand with credibility. Credibility is something that all leaders and potential leaders must aspire to obtain. Establishing credibility as a leader isn't something that happens instantly. It's a process that involves time, effort, and patience."

James M. Kouzes and Barry Z. Posner (2003), two of the world's leading experts on the importance of credibility and its relationship with leadership effectiveness, note, "Leadership is a reciprocal relationship between those who choose to lead and those who choose to follow. Any discussion of leadership must attend to the dynamics of this relationship" (p. 1). These authors claim that to establish this relationship between leader and follower, the leader must first establish the connection of moral purpose (Kouzes & Posner, 2003). A leader must possess the ability to connect his or her core values with his or her followers' values and then fuse them with the values of the organization. Establishing credibility begins with a leader clearly articulating what he or she stands for and stimulating that level of passion among followers. A school leader who is passionate about issues (such as equity or social justice) has to declare those passions, work to prove that others should find them important, and show that pursuing those passions will eventually benefit students. That commitment fuses leader and follower in moral purpose, establishing the leader as a trustworthy, moral, and ethical head of the movement.

Also, to establish leadership credibility, leaders must possess a deep knowledge of their craft. Followers want to know that the person leading them through change will guide them on the best course. Leaders who try to create change but have not established themselves as having intellectual authority do nothing but stimulate a power struggle. George N. Root III (n.d.) explains:

> A leader needs to have more than a basic understanding of his field to develop credibility with his staff, his customers and other companies within the industry. A leader is expected to be an expert in his field with the ability to analyze a situation and develop several potential solutions.

Displaying intellectualism marks an important stage in establishing credibility, but displaying reliability is equally essential. A leader's actions must match his or her words. A leader with a strong knowledge base does not impress followers if he or she does not follow up claims with congruent behavior. David Spungin (2015) declares that effective leaders have to walk their talk:

> Call it what you like; walking your talk, practice what you preach, put your money where your mouth is, or simply doing what you say you are going to do. They are all different ways of stating a fundamental leadership truth—a leader's credibility is a function of how well he or she follows through on his or her promises.

Leaders do not have to make great promises; they can promise something as simple as visiting a collaborative team meeting or delivering resources to teachers by a certain date. A leader has to view every promise as an opportunity to prove reliability. Over time, followers know that their leader has credibility with an established track record of words equaling action.

In the following sections, we present three scenarios designed to help you practice your ability to establish credibility to stimulate intrinsic commitment to change. As you review and reflect on each scenario, we want you to critically analyze your current philosophies and practices. Ask, "Are my current theories and practices aligned or are they incongruent?" "Do I establish trust with those I lead?" Consider the research and evidence presented in this chapter to guide your answers and responses. After each scenario, we provide some important considerations designed to help you reflect on your own thinking and habits as they relate to the research and the aim of each scenario.

WHO?

 ### SCENARIO ONE: *Transforming a Rebellious Staff*

You are the new principal at an elementary school. The teaching staff were enamored with the previous principal's warm personality. His commitment to listening to their concerns endeared him to them. The new district superintendent fired him because, although he was beloved, student academic performance declined over his five-year tenure, and a lot of parents and the local middle school complained that the school did not academically prepare students.

The school district invested heavily in the Professional Learning Communities at Work (PLC) process five years ago. The board of education arranged for early student dismissal every Wednesday so that teachers would have two hours of collaborative time. The district allotted nearly 50 percent of its professional development budget to invest in conferences and training where teachers would improve their skills in curriculum, assessment, and academic interventions to enhance the PLC process. All the other schools in the district demonstrated enormous gains in student achievement, but your elementary school showed a decline in the indicators of student academic achievement. It is well known that the former principal did not require teachers to attend their collaborative meetings and that he fabricated reports to the central office to give the appearance of compliance with district expectations. The staff admired the former principal's willingness to subvert district policy and protect them from systemic change, and ultimately changes in their professional practice.

You were hired because of your track record with and knowledge of the PLC process. You have extensively studied the process, and you truly believe in it. Your previous school was honored as a model PLC, and you are expected to stimulate the same level of PLC commitment at your new school and mirror the commitment throughout the school district. How would you establish yourself as a credible leader and create the trust necessary that will stimulate commitment to the PLC process among a staff that have been taught to rebel? Use figure 3.4 to reflect on this scenario and brainstorm strategies.

Scenario One: Transforming a Rebellious Staff	Strategies
How would you articulate your moral purpose and connect it to the change you propose?	• • •
How would you stimulate a moral connection between those you lead and the change you propose?	• • •
How would you display your knowledge, competence, and expertise in this area?	• • •
How would you establish your commitment to the process you are proposing and show that you are a consistent leader who "walks your talk"?	• • •

Figure 3.4: Strategies for transforming a rebellious staff.

*Visit **go.SolutionTree.com/leadership** for a free reproducible version of this figure.*

Consider the following when reflecting on this scenario.

▶ The school staff have a very incomplete understanding of the PLC at Work process. The process was never fully explained or modeled for them, so your insight, expertise, and experience can potentially change their view of the process.

▶ The school culture has been shaped to be duplicitous; people in the school profess one thing, but do something different. Your attention to integrity in thoughts, words, and deeds will go a long way in reshaping the established ineffective professional norm.

▶ Be careful not to throw the previous principal under the bus. Though he created some very unprofessional norms, the staff appreciated his warm personality. You can exhibit that same personal warmth while simultaneously modeling professionalism and ethical behavior.

SCENARIO TWO: *Dealing With Distrust and Pessimism*

You are the new reading coach at a middle school—the third reading coach this school has hired in two years. Your predecessors did not establish strong relationships with the school's teachers, and they rarely involved themselves in influencing the quality of reading instruction. You've heard the rumor from other reading coaches in the school district that they all behaved like quasi-administrators. School leadership used them to supervise students and respond to student discipline referrals instead of encouraging them to get deeply involved in improving student reading. You've also been told by teachers at your new school that the previous reading coaches did not possess backgrounds in reading instruction; rather, each one had a strong personal relationship with the principal, which is how they got the job—not because of their professional competence.

Your job description demands that you meet with teachers during their weekly collaborative time and observe them to provide insight into improving their reading instructional practices. After one month on the job, the principal starts to ask you to do things that have no relevance to your job description, like processing student disciplinary infractions. You start to understand the level of distrust and pessimism that the teachers have articulated. You have a passion for reading, and you want the teachers to embrace your passion for reading instruction and collaborate with you as their reading coach. How would you establish your credibility with the teachers, while redrawing your professional boundaries with the school principal? Use figure 3.5 (page 58) to reflect on this scenario and brainstorm strategies.

WHO?

Scenario Two: Dealing With Distrust and Pessimism	Strategies
How would you articulate your moral purpose and connect it to the change you propose?	• • •
How would you stimulate a moral connection between those you lead and the change you propose?	• • •
How would you display your knowledge, competence, and expertise in this area?	• • •
How would you establish your commitment to the process you are proposing and show that you are a consistent leader who "walks your talk"?	• • •

Figure 3.5: Strategies for dealing with distrust and pessimism.

*Visit **go.SolutionTree.com/leadership** for a free reproducible version of this figure.*

Consider the following when reflecting on this scenario.

▶ Consider inviting the principal to lunch or arranging a meeting to share your vision for your position. Perhaps the principal misunderstands the reading coach position and does not understand how to support the position.

▶ Consider co-teaching lessons with teachers to demonstrate the potential benefits of your ideas. Teachers can be great allies when trying to lobby for uninterrupted professional time. Perhaps, like the principal, the teachers are not convinced that a reading coach is helpful because of their experiences.

▶ Consider documenting the impact that your work is having on teachers and students. This might make the principal think twice about using your time for duties not in alignment with your purpose. You might also want to consider sharing that information and evidence with someone at the central office who might have to intervene if the evidence does not change the behavior of your principal.

SCENARIO THREE: *Fulfilling Promises*

You are the new school board president. Your school district, where you served as a classroom teacher before retiring, has experienced seven years of labor struggles. During the previous seven years, teachers' salaries were cut by 10 percent, and employee contributions to health insurance increased by 400 percent. This has greatly strained relationships between school staff and management, with school board meetings serving as regular sites for protests and emotional outbursts—all of which have appeared on local news channels.

You decided to run for school board president on a platform of *students first*. You gained the support of the local teachers' union and your former colleagues when you promised that you would place local students' needs at the forefront of the board's agenda and return resources to teachers so they can focus on educating the community's children. But you also empathize with the district's budgetary challenges.

After the election, you meet with the sitting board members and get access to the district's financial records. You recognize some wasted spending in nonacademic areas that the district could reallocate to the classroom so it provides a more resource-rich academic environment for both teachers and students. You are the only former educator on the school board. How do you establish your personal credibility with a board of education that lacks your educational and professional background and convince members to reprioritize their budget? How would you convince the union and teachers that you are a credible representative of their interests and that your campaign promises were not just rhetoric? Use figure 3.6 (page 60) to reflect on this scenario and brainstorm strategies.

Consider the following when reflecting on this scenario.

▸ Consider taking a few board members on a field trip to visit a classroom that has been greatly impacted by the budget cuts. This experience might help the board humanize their budget discussions and look beyond numbers.

▸ Provide insight on how the noninstructional expenditures, which you believe are wasteful, do not impact student achievement and are better spent in other ways. Consider using more than personal narratives; exposing the board to empirical educational research might establish your credibility and expertise.

WHO?

Scenario Three: Fulfilling Promises	Strategies
How would you articulate your moral purpose and connect it to the change you propose?	• • •
How would you stimulate a moral connection between those you lead and the change you propose?	• • •
How would you display your knowledge, competence, and expertise in this area?	• • •
How would you establish your commitment to the process you are proposing and show that you are a consistent leader who "walks the talk"?	• • •

Figure 3.6: Strategies for fulfilling promises.

*Visit **go.SolutionTree.com/leadership** for a free reproducible version of this figure.*

▸ Consider having a similar dialogue with the teachers' union about its priorities as they relate to research. This will show good faith and that the district agenda is making decisions that positively affect students.

Conclusion

Leaders who desire to transform their followers' behavior cannot ignore the emotional side of human nature. Making an intellectual or cognitive connection gets leaders off to a good start, but deep connections happen at an emotional level—they bind people with an organizational vision and answer the questions, Who? Are my leaders concerned about me as a person? Can I trust my leaders to guide us to success and organizational prosperity? Without trust between leaders and followers, no emotional connection will develop. When leaders display the essential elements of establishing trust—empathy and credibility—they show their character and competence, making connecting with those they lead possible. Use the rating scale in figure 3.7 to rate your proficiency in establishing trust.

Establishing Trust Rating Scale

Use the following rating scale to rate your proficiency in establishing trust in each of the skill areas.

1	2	3	4	5
Strongly Disagree				Strongly Agree

_____ I create opportunities to connect with and express deep concern about others' emotions.

_____ I listen, without rebuttal, to validate others' feelings, even if those feelings do not match my own.

_____ I collaborate with others to find a common resolution.

_____ I create opportunities to establish my core values and moral purpose and connect them to the values of those I lead.

_____ I create opportunities to demonstrate my deep knowledge, wisdom, and insight related to the proposed change.

_____ I prove that I have credibility by walking the talk.

Figure 3.7: Establishing trust rating scale.

*Visit **go.SolutionTree.com/leadership** for a free reproducible version of this figure.*

WHO?

4

Building Capacity: Making a Functional Investment

Confusion permeated the district-sponsored professional development training as yet another district initiative was introduced—this one to help all students read at grade level. Teachers had expected a different focus. Just three months earlier, when the district distributed the newly adopted curriculum for language arts, leaders promised that follow-up training would be available at this particular professional development day. That would not be the case.

To a great many teachers' surprise, a sales representative for the company that sold the new curriculum to the district (and admitted to only having had two years of teaching experience himself) spent a large chunk of the training day discussing how to supplement the curriculum to address the needs of English learners. While many teachers appreciated this focus, especially since English learners were a growing student cohort in the district, they all left with one very significant question in mind: How do we provide supplemental materials for students learning English as a second language if we still do not firmly grasp the intricacies of the core curriculum?

District and site leaders suggested teachers collaboratively read the teacher handbook and watch the training DVD that accompanied the new curriculum material. For the teachers, this suggestion added insult to injury. Teachers were frustrated and wondered if investing time to learn this new curriculum was even worth it if they would not receive the appropriate support from district leaders to be able to implement it with the fidelity required for success.

We have introduced two vital, equally important skills that transformational leaders must have to influence change in schools: (1) communicating why a particular change is needed, and (2) establishing trusting relationships with those they lead. When leaders have these two skills, it makes their followers more informed about a proposed change and the reason it is necessary, and the followers trust their leader to direct such a change. But if the followers lack the knowledge and expertise to actualize change—the how—leaders should expect resistance. Ronald A. Heifetz and Donald L. Laurie (1997) write, "Too often, leaders, their team, and consultants fail to identify and tackle the adaptive dimensions of the challenge and to ask themselves, Who needs to learn what in order to develop, understand, commit to, and implement the strategy?" (p. 133).

To put it simply, not knowing how to perform a specific task while simultaneously being held accountable for doing so makes the followers feel anxious and frustrated. As a result, a feeling of inadequacy emerges, creating a desire to join forces with others who also feel incapable and wish to rid the organization of the uncomfortable source of change (Muhammad, 2009). Transformational leaders must fuel their followers with the capacity to confidently perform the task at hand, because failure to do so will result in frustration that, over time, will produce resistance to change.

Leaders should not assume that people within the organization have the ability to produce a desired outcome simply because they have communicated the outcome to them. A military commander would not expect soldiers to carry out a military mission without adequate training. Coaches of a professional sports team would not expect players to win a national title without ever practicing and preparing for the championship game. Leaders must be cognizant of the knowledge and skills that those expected to carry out change initiatives require. Envisioned change does not become a reality until leaders identify an appropriate approach to developing human capital—providing the knowledge required to successfully accomplish a task (Brown & Duguid, 2000).

Building Capacity as a Leadership Skill

To assume that staff are prepared to do what leaders have communicated is comparable to gambling with the fate of the organization. Considering that actions adults take in schools will directly affect students' lives, school leaders must never assume the staff, as willing and eager as they may appear, are sufficiently prepared to implement necessary initiatives. In our work as educational consultants, we often initiate communication with school or district leaders prior to our arrival to make sure we set clear expectations regarding our services. Often, leaders make comments such as, "Our staff already know the basics, so feel free to take them to the next level," and once we begin interacting with participants, we discover that the leader's assessment was more assumption than fact. Kerry Patterson, Joseph Grenny, David Maxfield, Ron McMillan, and Al Switzler (2008) mirror our experience with schools when they state, "When leaders and training designers combine too much motivation with too few opportunities to improve ability, they don't produce change; they create resentment and depression. Influence masters (effective leaders) overinvest in strategies that help increase ability" (p. 112).

Leaders must learn to differentiate between exposing educators to best practice and ensuring that staff can actually carry out the specific knowledge and skills aligned with best practice. By no means do we downplay the fundamental importance of communicating the reason why a change initiative is important; instead, we advocate that transformational leaders couple their articulation of why with concrete plans for how those expected to navigate change can effectively execute it.

In his book *Leading in a Culture of Change*, Michael Fullan (2001) argues that effective leaders "commit themselves to constantly generating and increasing knowledge inside and outside the organization" (p. 6), and refers to the relationship between leader and follower as *knowledge building*. Likewise, transformational leaders tactfully and purposely provide those within the organization with concrete opportunities to discuss, learn, and apply knowledge and skills aimed at increasing the organization's productivity. Realizing this critical component of leadership supports those expected to execute change so they develop a sense of empowerment and confidence. This, in turn, fuels their human desire to make change happen—not because the leader tells them to do so, but because they understand why the change is needed and they feel equipped to successfully accomplish the task.

In *School Leadership That Works*, Robert J. Marzano, Timothy Waters, and Brian A. McNulty (2005) conduct a meta-analysis of thirty years of research and conclude that school leadership has a "substantial effect on student achievement and provides guidance for experienced and aspiring administrators alike" (p. 12). Marzano et al. (2005) introduce the twenty-one responsibilities of the school leader. Four of these responsibilities focus on building knowledge and skill capacity. Marzano et al. (2005) note that leaders have responsibility for:

1. **Intellectual stimulation**—Ensuring faculty and staff have awareness of the most current theories and practices and making the discussion of these a regular aspect of the school's culture

2. **Knowledge of curriculum, instruction, and assessment**—Maintaining awareness of current curriculum, instruction, and assessment practices

3. **Design and implementation of curriculum, instruction, and assessment—**Having direct involvement in designing and implementing curriculum, instruction, and assessment practices

4. **Resources—**Providing teachers with materials and professional development that they need to successfully execute their responsibilities

These attributes identify that effective leaders must not only build their own knowledge but also infuse knowledge throughout the organization. Consequently, both Fullan (2001) and Marzano and colleagues (2005) make it clear that school leaders who desire to change policies, practices, and procedures must ensure that those expected to carry out these changes acquire the knowledge and skills aligned with effective implementation.

A Bill and Melinda Gates Foundation (2014) report reveals that only 29 percent of teachers feel highly satisfied with their current professional development offerings and only 34 percent of teachers think professional development has improved. Relying on traditional "sit and get" professional development as the main approach to building schools' human capital is clearly not the best approach. Instead, teachers need to be invited to partake in the problem-solving process to engage in discussion about translating research and best practice into actual adult behaviors aligned with enhancing communicated school goals.

Similarly, district leaders interested in building principals' capacity to initiate and achieve organizational change might keep in mind that a MetLife (2013) report discloses 75 percent of principals feel the job has become too complex, and only four in ten principals say they have a great deal of control and confidence overseeing curriculum and instruction. In fact, in our work in schools, we weekly meet well-intentioned, hardworking principals who are held accountable by district leaders for increasing learning in their schools yet lack the fundamental knowledge and skills needed to successfully accomplish this goal. Consequently, whether transformational leaders expect teachers, principals, superintendents, or paraprofessionals to implement school change initiatives, they need to provide these stakeholders with concrete approaches to properly prepare them to successfully engage in change. Otherwise, it simply creates a recipe for failure.

Transformational leaders build others' capacity to achieve desired change initiatives through two actions: (1) generating the collective ability to problem solve and (2) creating a social context for learning.

Generating the Collective Ability to Problem Solve

Similar to the way in which children draw pictures by connecting numbered dots, transformational leaders help individuals connect the dots between why they need a change initiative and how a collaboratively discussed change will actually improve the organization. As we mentioned previously, schools are complex organizations that move at a fast pace. This makes it difficult for educators to find time to reflect. Effective leaders recognize the fast-paced context in which schools exist and find intentional ways to communicate why schools need change initiatives. Then they masterfully persuade others to connect and maneuver this newfound reasoning toward an action plan. Action plan development requires stakeholders within the organization to clearly define and redefine success so they can have a clear focus on the goal that leaders strive to achieve (Maxwell, 2007). Transformational school leaders do not decrease their momentum after the staff have embraced the reasons why an organization needs to change. In fact, quite the opposite is true. Transformational leaders pounce at this realization, gather members of the organization together, and tactfully discuss what specific actions the team will take to fuel the plan.

When school leaders effectively link the why and who aspects of change with a discussion centered on "What do we do next?" they formulate a more comprehensive vision of next steps. As our friend and colleague Timothy D. Kanold (2011) proposes, a leader has the key responsibility of "developing and delivering a compelling picture of the school's future that produces energy, passion, and action in yourself and others" (p. 6). Kouzes and Posner (2002) categorize this as a *forward-looking* leadership characteristic; it not only demonstrates concern for an organization's current state of affairs but also produces a host of possibilities moving forward. While we agree that effective school leaders create a vision of what must occur to accelerate a school or district's effectiveness, we contend that staff members will first require clarity between two points: (1) the organization's current reality and (2) the realization that they (not just the leader) must help formulate a plan of attack.

In chapter 2 (page 23), we introduced two skill sets that transformational leaders effectively utilize to make the case for why their organizations require change initiatives; they use (1) data and (2) persuasion to take action. Here, we contend that they need a space between data and persuasion in which creative cooperation (also known as *teamwork*) aims to find new solutions to old problems. Covey (1989) refers to this as *synergy*. As we often share with school leaders around the world, people will less likely tear down a fence they helped build. In other words, to cultivate a sense of determination and responsibility in those they expect to

HOW?

implement change, leaders will include stakeholders in developing the change initiative. Therefore, transformational leaders incorporate both collective ideas aimed at increasing the organization's productivity (Muhammad, 2009) and educational research, what we call *the science* of how educators improve learning in schools.

In the same manner that other professionals, such as doctors, civil engineers, and NASA astronauts, turn to the science of their professions (biology, calculus, and physics) to solve problems and strengthen critical facets of their organizations, transformational leaders in education infuse their schools with opportunities for staff to engage in research that aligns with best practice. As site principals with decades of experience, we learned that improving schools centers first and foremost on building shared knowledge (DuFour, DuFour, Eaker, Many, & Mattos, 2016). At Levey Middle School in Southfield, Michigan, where Anthony was principal, for example, site leadership unorthodoxly eliminated the mundane practice of sharing information easily accessible by other means (such as by hard-copy memos or emails) at faculty meetings. Instead, site leadership spent this team time researching and learning about practices that could help address aspects of the school that needed improvement. At Baldwin Park High School in Baldwin Park, California, where Luis was principal, site leadership initiated a process called *shared decision-making opportunity*. This process invites adult community members to take part in researching particular issues that negatively affect their school and then presenting recommendations to the entire staff for how best to move forward. Transformational leaders create a space where educators can become learners because they realize that when educators build shared knowledge based on educational research and collective experiences, persuading the faculty to commit to action becomes much more plausible (Patterson et al., 2002). Transformational leaders then align the rearticulated reasons why the organization must change with the responsibility of finding the knowledge and skill set relevant to its particular situation.

In the following sections, we present three scenarios designed to help you practice your ability to build capacity. As you review and reflect on each scenario, we want you to critically analyze your current philosophies and practices. Ask, "Are my current theories and practices aligned or are they incongruent?" and "Have I provided those I lead the necessary knowledge and skills to effectively implement change?" Consider the research and evidence presented in this chapter to guide your answers and responses. After each scenario, we provide some important considerations designed to help you reflect on your own thinking and habits as they relate to the research and the aim of each scenario.

SCENARIO ONE: *Promoting Collective Problem Solving*

You are the new superintendent of an urban school district. The board of education unanimously voted to hire you so you can increase evidence of learning as measured on state assessments. State department officials have warned the district that it is on the verge of going on a watch list for underperforming school districts if it does not produce evidence of student achievement in the next several years. When you meet the twelve principals from the district's schools, it pleases you to discover that seven of them demonstrate a sincere concern for the lack of student achievement plaguing their schools. One principal has actually achieved the unique distinction of *high achieving* as a result of strong evidence of student achievement on the last round of state exams. Upon inquiring further, you learn that this particular principal has established a strong collaborative culture for teachers. The principal has implemented both the PLC process and response to intervention (RTI), which are major reasons why student learning has flourished. When you ask other principals how well versed they are in PLC and RTI processes, their answers reveal limited awareness.

You begin your tenure as superintendent by sharing data with the principals, explaining what warrants change in policies, practices, and procedures. You share the board of education's goals and reasons why you were hired, and over time, you establish trustworthy relationships with the principals. The principals appreciate the support you provide them and begin to view you as a confident and credible leader. You realize that while healthy relationships are important, you must leverage the positivity of your relationships so you can train your principals on PLC and RTI processes that could elevate student learning across the district. How would you, as a first-year superintendent, promote collective problem-solving processes to empower your principals with the knowledge and skills they need to amplify student learning at each site? Use figure 4.1 (page 70) to reflect on this scenario and brainstorm strategies.

Consider the following when reflecting on this scenario.

▶ Sometimes, as leaders, we assume that what is obvious to us should be obvious to others. Consider using data across schools to generate a collective conversation focused on analyzing what it is that may be working at one school that is not working at others.

HOW?

Scenario One: Promoting Collective Problem Solving	Strategies
How would you build momentum toward collectively addressing shared challenges?	• • •
What resources would you use to formulate a healthy sense of professional curiosity toward possible solutions?	• • •
What research would you use to complement the collaborative solutions that staff generate?	• • •
How would you promote the transition from learning to applying?	• • •

Figure 4.1: Strategies for promoting collective problem solving.

*Visit **go.SolutionTree.com/leadership** for a free reproducible version of this figure.*

▶ How might you intentionally promote the transition from discussion to action planning? After reaching consensus on key findings based on the analysis of data, consider placing the responsibility of creating action plans on stakeholders to initiate desired change so that they have a voice in the problem-solving process.

▶ Consider promoting the importance of including other stakeholders (in this case, teachers) back at each site as part of the site action plan and encouraging an additional team approach to problem solving. Leaders need to be reminded that *people are less likely to tear down a fence they help build!*

SCENARIO TWO: *Sharing Instructional Techniques*

You are a veteran teacher with twenty years of experience at the elementary level. You have decided to expand your horizons and are hired to teach high school English. While the English department is welcoming, considering you have no experience teaching high school students, you make note that your team has apprehension regarding your addition to the team. You soon discover that your new team meets regularly to create, implement, and analyze common assessments. Over time, department members are impressed with the data that show your students have excelled academically. The previous year, the principal initiated weekly instructional rounds, a process whereby teachers observe each other's instruction to generate professional development. After several weeks of observing colleagues, you realize that your peers mostly lecture when they teach, whereas your years of elementary-level teaching have prepared you to create an engaging learning environment using additional instructional strategies. At the last team meeting, common assessment data revealed that 26 percent more of your students had proficiency than those taught by your peers.

Frequent data analysis has allowed you to share with your colleagues the instructional methods you effectively use to produce student learning. However, you notice that your colleagues usually listen and congratulate you by saying, "Nice job," but rarely demonstrate a sincere desire to learn your instructional delivery techniques. While it pleases you that your students have benefited from your teaching practices, your peers' lack of student achievement concerns you. Over time, it becomes clear to you that your colleagues' inability to implement effective teaching strategies stems more from a lack of capacity than from a negative attitude. How would you initiate a process whereby your peers can begin to learn and implement instructional practices more conducive to student achievement? Use figure 4.2 to reflect on this scenario and brainstorm strategies.

Scenario Two: Sharing Instructional Techniques	Strategies
How would you build momentum toward collectively addressing shared challenges?	• • •
What resources would you use to formulate a healthy sense of professional curiosity toward possible solutions?	• • •
What research would you use to complement the collaborative solutions that staff generate?	• • •
How would you promote the transition from learning to applying?	• • •

Figure 4.2: Strategies for sharing instructional techniques.

*Visit **go.SolutionTree.com/leadership** for a free reproducible version of this figure.*

HOW?

Consider the following when reflecting on this scenario.

▶ Remember that leadership is not just position but an action, a verb and a noun. Be keenly aware of when you can exchange established credibility for the attention of others to generate a sense of collective problem solving.

▶ Transformational leaders take tactful initiative to generate desired outcomes. Keep in mind that the prerequisite to collective problem solving is first courageously communicating the need to come together to explore an array of options to achieve better outcomes.

▶ Sometimes generating the collective ability for a team to resolve an issue is a gradual process. Might the teacher leader in question seek a partnership with a fellow peer first so that over time both may act as a resource for reaching the entire team?

SCENARIO THREE: *Instituting a Support System*

Over the past ten years, the number of students learning English as a second language at the middle school where you are principal has more than doubled. In 2008, 8 percent of your students were learning English as a second language; in 2018, that percentage has reached 22 percent. School district trends predict that next school year, at least a quarter of your students will be designated as English learners.

For seven years, your school was designated the highest-achieving middle school in the district, twice earning you the Principal of the Year distinction. You have established credible and trustworthy relationships with most staff members and decide the time has come to address the challenge of the increasing number of English learners. You prepare a detailed data presentation showcasing the demographic shifts in your community. School leadership team members share that the staff are becoming more frustrated due to their inability to produce tangible evidence of student achievement and are concerned that staff morale will deteriorate.

You realize that your hardworking staff, while experienced, lack the knowledge and skills to effectively meet the academic needs of English learners. In addition, the demographic shifts you have shared with the staff reveal that within the next five years, English learners will compose over half the student population. How would you, as the principal, initiate a process that would ensure your staff develop the knowledge and skills to best meet this emerging student cohort's needs? Use figure 4.3 to reflect on this scenario and brainstorm strategies.

Scenario Three: Instituting a Support System	Strategies
How would you build momentum toward collectively addressing shared challenges?	• • •
What resources would you use to formulate a healthy sense of professional curiosity toward possible solutions?	• • •
What research would you use to complement the collaborative solutions that staff generate?	• • •
How would you promote the transition from learning to applying?	• • •

Figure 4.3: Strategies for instituting a support system.

*Visit **go.SolutionTree.com/leadership** for a free reproducible version of this figure.*

Consider the following when reflecting on this scenario.

▶ Why not use the credibility and respect earned as a leader in exchange for a collective analysis of the reason why the staff are currently struggling with meeting the needs of this emerging student cohort? By collectively verifying that the challenge the staff face stems from a lack of skill rather than a lack of will, you may generate a more optimistic approach to solving this dilemma.

▶ Consider initiating a task force of teachers along with some administrators to begin to explore and share with the faculty research-based approaches aimed at learning how best to meet the needs of English learners. If teachers help take the lead on exploring new techniques designed to address a particular challenge, then maybe other teachers will be more willing to listen and apply these skills.

▶ If, as they say, *seeing is believing*, why not consider collectively searching for schools achieving success with English learners and visit these schools as a team so that you can begin to formulate a more

HOW?

collective and detailed action plan. Remember that transformational leaders help paint a vision of what is possible.

While leaders may not have all the answers to challenges their schools face, the ability to bring others together for the purpose of generating not only ideas but a sense of comradery and direction is an essential skill that transformational leaders must develop over time. A commitment to action is more plausible when those expected to carry out change initiatives have had a voice in the process. The intellectual stimuli transformational leaders initiate when they embrace collective problem-solving approaches bridge the gap between discovering what to do and actually formulating a plan to move forward. Therefore, processes intended to include a collective approach toward problem solving must be coupled with creating a social context for learning.

Creating a Social Context for Learning

Once transformational leaders actively include some staff in determining the knowledge and skills that all the staff need to meet organizational goals, the next challenge involves generating the right conditions so the remaining organization members learn. To generate commitment to actions meant to change critical aspects of the school, transformational leaders must first develop the precise setting where individuals can gain a collective aptitude to do the right work. This must take place in a setting in which learners engage socially (Fullan, 2001). In other words, those expected to carry out change must not only hear the details surrounding the change but actually learn all the complexities of implementing change initiatives. Fullan (2001) writes:

> Incidentally, focusing on information rather than use is why sending individuals and even teams to external training by itself does not work. Leading in a culture of change does not mean placing changed individuals into unchanged environments. Rather, change leaders work on changing the context, helping create new settings conducive to learning and sharing that learning. (p. 79)

Transformational leaders intentionally create environments in which people vehemently grapple with comprehension and application of new knowledge and skills. They do this not to create frustration but instead to create a sense of empowerment.

Therefore, it is critical that transformational leaders themselves learn what constitutes an effective learning environment for the adults in their schools or districts and, as a result, reflect on questions such as:

▶ In what setting (an auditorium, a small room, and so on) will training for organization members take place?

▶ Who will have responsibility for providing this training, and does this individual possess the credibility needed to build trust in those receiving the training?

▶ How will the training be provided, and will this approach allow those receiving the training to interact with each other to build consensus, which simultaneously builds a social web of learning (an opportunity for interactions between people to accentuate desired learning)?

▶ How will the training allow feedback and reflection time between and among participants so as to allow further focus on exploring best options for school improvement?

▶ Will the training be coupled with additional support in the form of coaching to further support those tasked with the responsibility to implement desired changes?

The Learning Policy Institute report *Effective Teacher Professional Development* identifies elements of structured professional learning that result in changed teacher practices and improved student learning outcomes (Darling-Hammond, Hyler, & Gardner, 2017). The report's authors find the following seven elements of professional development most effective for increasing teachers' capacity (Darling-Hammond et al., 2017). The professional development:

1. Is content focused, meaning teaching strategies align with specific curriculum

2. Incorporates active learning for teachers, allowing them to design and try out teaching strategies

3. Supports collaboration among teachers, allowing for a space where teachers can exchange ideas

4. Uses models of effective practice and peer observations

5. Provides coaching and expert support, which addresses teachers' individual needs

HOW?

6. Offers feedback and reflection, allowing teachers to reflect and engage in conversations aimed at strengthening their practice

7. Has a sustained duration, allowing sufficient time for teachers to actively learn, practice, implement, and reflect on new strategies that facilitate change in practice

Andy Hargreaves and Michael Fullan (2012) believe that the "combination of these elements creates a collaborative culture that results in a form of collective professional capital that leverages much more productive, widespread improvement in an organization than would be possible if teachers worked alone in egg-crate classrooms" (p. 23). While this particular research focuses on teacher outcomes, we have witnessed the same high level of knowledge production with other school and district employees with whom we have worked as consultants. When district leaders, site principals, support staff, and board members, for example, have the opportunity to intellectually grapple with such elements of professional development, they develop more concrete knowledge and skills. A sense of ownership and empowerment also begins to take hold, creating interest and intrigue in what they are learning. Transformational leaders master the ability to initiate the right degree of discussion that empowers key organization members to take action. When transformational leaders create a social context where participants share, discuss, model, debate, and eventually agree, the group develops confidence and efficacy. Within the transition from leaders presenting knowledge to participants embracing that knowledge, transformational leaders tap into the human potential necessary to increase productivity and create successful change.

In the following sections, we present three scenarios designed to help you practice your ability to create a social context for learning. As you review and reflect on each scenario, we want you to critically analyze your current philosophies and practices. Ask, "Are my current theories and practices aligned or are they incongruent?" and "Have I provided those I lead the necessary knowledge and skills to effectively implement change?" Consider the research and evidence presented in this chapter to guide your answers and responses. After each scenario, we provide some important considerations designed to help you reflect on your own thinking and habits as they relate to the research and the aim of each scenario.

SCENARIO ONE: *Designing Meeting Time*

After one year as superintendent, you are pleased to learn that your leadership style has generated a strong sense of trust and credibility among a majority of stakeholders throughout the district. An anonymous survey of site principals regarding your performance as superintendent has revealed that 92 percent of respondents trust your intentions as leader and, as a result, find you very credible. In addition, the survey reveals that your intentional approach to gathering and discussing data relevant to student achievement has persuaded principals to embrace professional curiosity toward unveiling possible ways they could increase student learning schoolwide. You realize that the political context for change is ideal and decide that investing in sending principals to conferences on helping teachers improve their instructional delivery would meet with very little resistance. In addition, you invest thousands of dollars in building a professional library that displays some of the most current research aligned with increasing student achievement, and you encourage principals to invest in bringing consultants to their schools to add yet another layer of professional development. You also passionately promote administrative book circles as an avenue for learning.

After one year of supporting principals in this manner, district-generated benchmarks show very little growth in student achievement, and even though you promoted administrative book circles, you noticed many principals stopped checking out books halfway through the year. This reality makes you question whether the tradition of using principal meeting time to discuss management and compliance matters needs to change. How would you, as superintendent, design principals' meeting time so they learn best practice and generate action plans for effective implementation of what they have learned? Use figure 4.4 (page 78) to reflect on this scenario and brainstorm strategies.

Consider the following when reflecting on this scenario.

▶ Remember that while exposing principals to research-based literature is a step in the right direction, it is not enough. It will be important to discuss and challenge ideas generated from reading to initiate the process of bridging what we learn with practical implementation.

▶ Might it be time to find an alternative way of communicating management aspects of being a principal to provide ample time and space to invest in learning research-based practices designed to enhance student learning? What might these new structures look like?

▶ What if, in addition to rich conversations regarding research-based strategies, we also regularly include at our meetings guest speakers who have experienced both successes and failures associated with implementation of these ideas? How might this approach further solidify for principals the need to create action plans based on what is being learned?

HOW?

Scenario One: Designing Meeting Time	Strategies
How would you create a process that incorporates collaboration between stakeholders as an essential component of learning and implementation of best practice?	• • •
How would you incorporate peer observation and discussion as integral aspects of learning and implementation?	• • •
Would you consider initiating a coaching approach to generate learning, and if so, what steps would you take to do so?	• • •
What practices would you incorporate to include feedback and reflection in the learning process?	• • •

Figure 4.4: Strategies for designing meeting time.

*Visit **go.SolutionTree.com/leadership** for a free reproducible version of this figure.*

SCENARIO TWO: *Impacting Long-Held Practices*

As a second-year coordinator of your school district's English learner programs, you are pleased to reflect on the positive strides the district has made in supporting students learning English as a second language. The partnership among your department, human resources, and the school budget office allowed for a 20 percent increase in the number of bilingual paraprofessionals hired to work in classrooms that serve high numbers of English learners. The following year, you successfully convinced the education services office to invest an additional fifty thousand dollars so the new language arts textbook included supplemental curriculum and technology resources for teachers serving English learners. This generated sincere accolades throughout the district. Likewise, your districtwide implementation of multilingual parent workshops has garnered public praise at board meetings, where participants compliment your insight and leadership. You feel confident that although persuading teachers to change how they interact with students learning English will be difficult, this is an important next step to employ.

For years, the district has assigned the responsibility for coordinating English learner issues to a teacher volunteer on site. You have observed that this individual mostly addresses compliance issues, such as coordinating state testing for English learners and creating schedules that allot English learners computer lab time. Unfortunately, very little of the professional development you have presented to teachers in the past receives follow-up. In fact, the teacher volunteer usually only informs the faculty of practices they should adhere to based on past trainings from a memo you send regarding a reminder of best instructional practices. As a result, teachers lack the knowledge and skills that will best serve English learners. How would you systematically begin to change the current process for educating teachers of English learners? Use figure 4.5 to reflect on this scenario and brainstorm strategies.

Scenario Two: Impacting Long-Held Practices	Strategies
How would you create a process that incorporates collaboration between stakeholders as an essential component of learning and implementation of best practice?	• • •
How would you incorporate peer observation and discussion as integral aspects of learning and implementation?	• • •
Would you consider initiating a coaching approach to generate learning, and if so, what steps would you take to do so?	• • •
What practices would you incorporate to include feedback and reflection in the learning process?	• • •

Figure 4.5: Strategies for impacting long-held practices.

*Visit **go.SolutionTree.com/leadership** for a free reproducible version of this figure.*

Consider the following when reflecting on this scenario.

▶ Since clarity precedes competence, might there be a lack of understanding about expectations on the part of the teacher volunteer? How might you more effectively communicate your expectations for follow-up on past training?

> ▶ Sometimes leaving the responsibility for practical follow-up in the
> hands of one person rather than a team limits what actually gets done.
> What if instead of working through a person, you work through a
> team to meet your expected outcomes?

> ▶ Do you depend too much on someone else to communicate your
> expectations? How might one play a more direct role with those
> expected to implement specific stated expectations?

SCENARIO THREE: *Engaging Parents*

You beam with pride at the end-of-year employee recognition dinner as you receive the award for District Teacher of the Year: Teacher on Special Assignment. As the teacher on special assignment overseeing parent involvement in the district's largest elementary school, which serves a mostly low-income community, you have gotten appreciation and praise.

Board members especially have expressed their gratitude to you for making the diverse parent population always feel welcomed. At the ceremony, parents themselves present you with a card and cake to demonstrate their gratitude for the unconditional support that you provide them and their children on a daily basis.

You reflect on the past year's accomplishments, and the communication that you have initiated with parents especially pleases you. Your parent newsletter, which you send home once a month, has kept parents abreast not just of school events but of data pertinent to student achievement. It gives parents advice regarding how they can support learning at home. Upon realizing that you needed to do more than simply provide advice via the newsletter, you initiated monthly parent workshops. These workshops, held in both the morning and evening, initially generated much interest from parents. Unfortunately, you have noticed that each month, the number of parents participating in both the morning and evening workshops significantly declines. When you surveyed parents about the workshops' quality, 76 percent of respondents indicated that while they appreciated the opportunity, they found it difficult to understand the guest presenters (many of whom lectured via PowerPoint using terms unfamiliar to parents). And 83 percent of parent respondents found the workshops "nonmotivating"; in other words, they found them boring!

You know that the credibility you have established as an effective teacher on special assignment has paved the way so you can influence parents to embrace their partnership with teachers and increase student achievement. How would you create a more effective learning environment for parents that focuses on acquisition of the knowledge and skills that can promote their children's learning? Use figure 4.6 to reflect on this scenario and brainstorm strategies.

Scenario Three: Engaging Parents	Strategies
How would you create a process that incorporates collaboration between stakeholders as an essential component of learning and implementation of best practice?	• • •
How would you create structures that allow stakeholders to connect with one another as sources of continuous support?	• • •
Would you consider initiating a mentor approach to generate learning, and if so, what steps would you take to do so?	• • •
What practices would you incorporate to include feedback and reflection in the learning process?	• • •

Figure 4.6: Strategies for engaging parents.

Visit **go.SolutionTree.com/leadership** *for a free reproducible version of this figure.*

Consider the following when reflecting on this scenario.

▸ Develop a strong ability to read your audience. The same approach for learning you use with teachers may not work with parents. How might a different way of presenting information to parents be more effective?

▸ Consider searching for parents who have a reputation for effectively promoting academic success with their children. Might these parents be able to train less-experienced parents? What kind of relationship between more- and less-experienced parents could you use as leverage for promoting student success?

▸ Since parents do not work in schools and see each other on a daily basis, they may not have many opportunities to build relationships with one another that may prove to be important resources toward learning. How might you create structures conducive to long-lasting supportive parent relationships?

HOW?

Conclusion

Leaders who desire to transform their organizations so they achieve higher levels of student success must create environments conducive to learning for the adults they expect to carry out change. People will resist change when they do not have the knowledge or skills to successfully implement it. Leaders often make false assumptions regarding the degree of knowledge and skill that individuals have and, as a result, assume that an inability to embrace change indicates a lack of will, rather than the absence of skill. Effective leaders invite those expected to embrace and implement change to collectively study a problem and produce viable solutions. This generates a sense of empowerment and ownership in knowledge and skill acquisition. In short, leaders generate a healthy sense of professional curiosity aimed at improving outcomes. In addition, transformational leaders are keenly aware of the social dynamic that individuals must experience to confidently learn how to execute desired change initiatives. If leaders fail to create environments conducive to learning new ways of conducting business, their organizations will ultimately fail to move forward. Use the rating scale in figure 4.7 to rate your proficiency in building capacity.

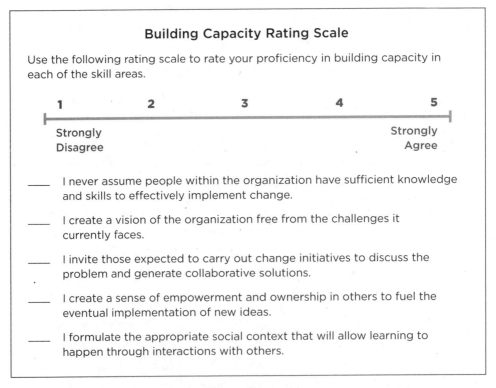

Figure 4.7: Building capacity rating scale.

*Visit **go.SolutionTree.com/leadership** for a free reproducible version of this figure.*

5

Getting Results:
Collecting the Return on Investment

The second-year high school principal racked her brain, attempting to identify what kind of support she had failed to provide her teachers. She spent her entire first year as principal establishing trustworthy relationships, formulating a school leadership team made up of many seasoned and well-respected teachers, and presenting data to the staff that lead to consensus on the need to address the learning needs of students with disabilities. In addition, the staff survey she initiated with the leadership team revealed the type of training teachers desired to address the learning needs. In response to the survey, the principal used site monies to fund research-based training, and, as a result, talented trainers, which the majority of the staff requested, regularly provided enriching professional development. Yet, despite this investment in resources for teachers to meet the needs of students with disabilities, the state summative assessment data revealed very little growth for this critical student population.

Determined to find answers, the principal decided that asking the teachers on the leadership team to provide some guidance was her best bet. Upon sharing her frustration with the team, she was dumbfounded at the teachers' hesitance to speak to her concerns.

"Am I not providing enough support?" asked the principal.

"You are providing more support than we have ever received," replied a veteran teacher on the team.

"Then what could it be?" the principal replied.

Finally, a teacher on the team spoke up: "To put it simply, a lot of teachers have chosen not to implement what we have learned because of their discomfort with what the training states is required."

It was at that moment that the principal realized she had failed to actively foster a return on her investment.

DO!

83

Up to this point, we have explored the first three parts of the Why? Who? How? Do! model that we present in the introduction (page 1). Leaders have clearly communicated the rationale for why a change is logical and essential (cognitive investment), established a trusting relationship with those they lead (emotional investment), and provided extensive training and resources so followers can effectively execute the change (functional investment). What remains is the action—completing the task or implementing the plan to make the desired results a reality. As we said earlier, this moment when action can take place marks the tipping point between support and accountability. Once leaders have made their investments, they can logically expect a return on those investments.

We have also expressed that leaders need to remain cognizant of the emotional complexities involved when people face the need to embrace change initiatives. If leaders have paid close attention to the why, who, and how, and made the appropriate cognitive, emotional, and functional investments, most individuals will respond rationally and move into action. When leaders fail to make the necessary investments, however, it amplifies the possibility of resistance to change, and it is rational for followers to resist under these circumstances.

The skills we have outlined will sufficiently help leaders get results with most individuals. However, some individuals may still refuse to embrace change initiatives regardless of the supportive measures that leaders have taken. While a lack of support produces rational resistance to change, the unwillingness to respond to the support that leaders provide indicates an irrational resistance to change. Transformational leaders realize and accept the unfortunate reality that certain organization members will irrationally resist getting on board with change regardless of the amount of support they receive. As a result, leaders need to hold these members directly accountable for performing the behaviors aligned to the change initiative. This revelation will prompt the leader to transition from provider of support to initiator of intentional and direct accountability. At this point, leaders must tactfully articulate the following message: "The support provided thus far is not a request for you to embrace change. It is an expectation that you do so."

Getting Results as a Leadership Skill

As former teachers and school-site administrators, we can attest that educators have negative connotations of accountability. The first sentence in Douglas B. Reeves's (2004) book *Accountability for Learning: How Teachers and School Leaders Can Take Charge*, for example, says this: "For many educators, *accountability* has become a dirty word" (p. 5). Indeed, people often associate accountability with images of Big Brother micromanaging hardworking educators while simultaneously disseminating insensitive repercussions for not meeting expectations. *Merriam-Webster's Online Dictionary* defines *accountability* as "an obligation or willingness to accept responsibility or to account for one's actions" ("Accountability," n.d.). While we agree that school leaders must account for the actions they expect of school personnel, note that holding others accountable for desired behaviors includes a wide gamut of approaches. These approaches begin with understanding the difference between creating a culture of accountability and holding others accountable. When transformational leaders help formulate a culture of accountability, most people within the organization understand why a change is needed, trust those initiating the change initiative, and know what they must do to implement the proposed change. These individuals will embrace the proposed initiative and, as a result, motivate themselves and others to implement the desired change.

Reeves (2004) supports our insight toward creating a culture of accountability with what he calls *holistic approaches to accountability*. When leaders view accountability through a holistic lens, school staff examine not just summative student learning results (for example, end-of-year test scores) but also approaches they may use (curriculum, teaching practices, and leadership practices) to improve student academic performance. In doing so, they generate a sense of collective curiosity and discovery that leads to the best conditions a staff require to become motivated to embrace change initiatives. This sense of collective motivation, in turn, creates a culture of accountability—a professional attitude whereby peers respectfully hold one another accountable for collectively developed and agreed-on actions. Patrick Lencioni (2005), like Reeves (2004), also couples accountability with the potential for collective motivation when he writes, "Peer pressure and the distaste for letting down a colleague will motivate a team player more than any fear of authoritative punishment or rebuke" (p. 61).

Kanold (2011) links accountability with an organization's responsibility to celebrate when he writes:

> In other words, through accountability and celebration, you lead the transition from vision to realized action and implementation. As you grow in this discipline, you will learn to strike a balance between accountability and celebration, both of which are necessary to sustain continuous improvement. (p. 7)

Celebrating accomplishments sends a subtle yet powerful message to members of an organization: *What we are trying to do is so vital to our purpose as a school, that we are willing to make time to honor and acknowledge those who have contributed to our goals.* As a result, two positive outcomes occur. First, those members of the organization following through with implementation of change initiatives are motivated to continue to strive in this direction. Second, those members of the organization who have not committed to aligning their behaviors to organizational goals are indirectly reminded that the expectation to do so remains.

Organizational research, including research on school systems, validates the critical importance of developing a culture of accountability when promoting school change initiatives. The skill sets we have introduced thus far focus on communicating the rationale, establishing trust, and building capacity, which all contribute to a culture of accountability in which transformational leaders empower those they lead to have accountability for agreed-on behaviors. Transformational leaders need these important skills to create a culture of accountability; however, equally important is the skill set that leaders must be prepared to use so they can hold individuals directly accountable if they fail to hold themselves accountable. These two skills include (1) using tactful confrontation and (2) using professional monitoring.

Using Tactful Confrontation

Lencioni (2005) contributes to the general understanding of accountability as a collective responsibility, one that extends beyond the obligation of the team leader or, in the case of schools, the administrator. He writes, "I define accountability as the willingness of team members to remind one another when they are not living up to the performance standards of the group" (Lencioni, 2005, p. 61). In addition, he reveals the critical importance of leaders' willingness to address behaviors that contribute to poor results when he writes:

> But most leaders I know have a far easier time holding people accountable for their results than they do for behavioral issues. This is a problem because behavioral problems almost always precede results. That means team members have to be willing to call each other on behavioral issues, as uncomfortable as that might be, and if they see their leaders balk at doing this, then they aren't going to do it themselves. (Lencioni, 2005, p. 61)

Indeed, in our combined over thirty years of experience as public school educators, we have witnessed well-intentioned school leaders focus their efforts more on a lack of desired results than on behaviors directly linked to poor performance. In the following examples, leaders choose to address outcomes rather than behaviors, contributing to those outcomes that we have observed over the years.

- An elementary school principal addresses the entire staff with data revealing that the school's students have the lowest reading scores in the district. However, the principal fails to confront the reality that teacher teams throughout the school rarely use the data and intervention systems designed to support students who read below grade level, even though the school has invested significantly in training the teachers to do so.

- A middle school leadership team reveals to the staff that students demonstrated dismal mathematics performance on the district-initiated midyear assessment. The team proclaims, "We need our students to do better," but fails to discuss that few mathematics teachers at the school are using the district-recommended mathematics curriculum, which focuses on rigor. According to conversations the team has overheard in the teachers' lounge, "The curriculum is just too hard for our students."

- A high school science department chair shares with her colleagues the bleak results of a common assessment, which focused on critical aspects of an essential standard, that they all agreed to use. However, she doesn't discuss that when she had the opportunity to observe her colleagues as they taught the essential standard, she witnessed them teaching mostly ineffectively with little, if any, student engagement. She does not discuss what she observed with teachers because, as she says, "It's not my place to discuss how teachers teach."

- A district English learner director meets with principals to discuss the growing number of students learning English as a second language who are not reaching fluency. He shares programs with the principals that they can purchase to help English learners. However, he does not discuss the fact that the principals fail to hold teachers accountable when they do not incorporate the district-sponsored English learner instructional training into their teaching.

Leaders' direct or indirect refusal to address adult behavior limits improvement. Because these leaders feel uncomfortable with or avoid conflict, they have to accept responsibility for poor outcomes. Just as financial investors expect and, if need be, demand results for their monetary investments, transformational leaders do not hesitate to tactfully confront individuals whose behavior undermines their investments.

DO!

In their best-selling book *Crucial Confrontations: Tools for Resolving Broken Promises, Violated Expectations, and Bad Behavior*, Patterson and his colleagues (2005) define *confrontation* as "holding someone accountable, face to face" (p. 4) and offer six steps for confronting others regarding behaviors that warrant a behavioral change.

1. **Choose *what* and *if*:** Those preparing to confront others must first clarify and focus on the exact "content, pattern, or relationship" (Patterson et al., 2005, p. 218) of the behavior that lies at the core of the conflict. They must clarify the risks that not initiating the confrontation may bring.

2. **Master the stories:** Resist the desire to assume why a certain undesirable behavior is taking place. Instead, create the conditions for the "rest of the story"—clarity regarding what the individuals expressed happened—to be told (Patterson et al., 2005, p. 218).

3. **Describe the gap:** Start the actual conversation with facts that describe the disparity between desired and observed behaviors, and then end with a question to begin to diagnose the discrepancy. For example, "So you are saying that you did not follow through because of a lack of time?"

4. **Make it motivating and easy:** After the diagnosis, determine whether the individual's inability to apply the expected behavior stems from a lack of motivation, a lack of skill, or both. This analysis will inform the person who initiated the confrontation how best to proceed.

5. **Agree on a plan and follow up:** Articulate an action plan, and make sure both parties clearly know "who will do what by when with follow-up" (Patterson et al., 2005, p. 205).

6. **Stay focused and flexible:** Remain focused on making sure that what was articulated and discussed in step 5 actually happens. If it does not, be prepared to initiate a new crucial confrontation.

Patterson and his colleagues (2005) offer comprehensive, research-based approaches to initiating confrontations, key human interactions that are necessary to increase productivity in complex and ever-evolving organizations such as schools. In addition, we advocate that transformational leaders, whom others expect to enhance critical aspects of the organizations they represent, need to not only initiate confrontations when necessary but also have the ability to effectively do so. Unfortunately, while vast research has centered on accountability and steps that leaders should initiate when attempting to hold others accountable, in reality, few school leaders have received training on the skill of initiating and conducting tactful confrontations. A study conducted in Fort Worth, Texas (Anderson, 2007), for example, finds that while 91 percent of principals and assistant principals indicated that, based on their experience as site administrators, conflict-management skills are very important (another 7 percent of respondents identified conflict-management skills as important), only 45 percent of respondents indicated they had received some or limited conflict-management training from their university courses. Moreover, 26 percent of respondents indicated little to no such training from their university courses. When respondents considered the extent of school district training on conflict management that they received, less than half indicated extensive or considerable training (Anderson, 2007). Our work as educational consultants in schools around the world validates the often-articulated challenge that most site administrators have with either initiating or conducting tactful confrontations intended to hold others accountable. Furthermore, while we believe site administrators should not have sole responsibility for transformational leadership in schools, we find that when teachers and support staff take on leadership roles and lack the preparation and training to handle adult resistance to change, it amplifies the difficulties that administrators demonstrate in initiating or conducting tactful confrontations.

Steven J. Andelson (2001) and a team of attorneys from a law firm based in Cerritos, California, provide site administrators with a handbook that focuses on practical guidelines for documenting unsatisfactory employee performance. These five guidelines, represented by the acronym FRISK, present action steps that administrators should use for evaluation.

1. **Facts:** Present evidence of the employee's unsatisfactory conduct.

2. **Rule:** Note the rule or authority that the unsatisfactory conduct violated.

3. **Impact:** Describe the impact of the employee's unsatisfactory conduct on the district.

4. **Suggestions:** Provide suggestions that assist the employee in improving his or her performance, and provide direction about the proper conduct that you expect the employee to follow in the future.

DO!

5. **Knowledge:** Be aware of the employee's right to respond to derogatory information, such as a report of insubordination placed in his or her personnel file by an administrator, as state education code requires.

While administrators mainly use FRISK to initiate due process when formally disciplining employees, it is worth noting that the method directly addresses accountability. We therefore acknowledge both Andelson (2001) and Patterson et al.'s (2005) approaches to initiating confrontations and blend them to offer the following approach. Transformational leaders can consider it when they find that they need to tactfully confront an individual whose behavior contradicts a desired change initiative. Considering that we advocate that transformational leaders resist ignoring irrational resistance, we use the acronym RESIST to elaborate on the previously stated six-step approach to initiating tactful confrontation.

1. **Recognize** that failure to confront an individual regarding the behavior (or lack of behavior) that interferes with meeting a previously discussed objective communicates to that individual and other organization members that you accept counterproductive behaviors.

2. **Evaluate** whether the individual has received sufficient support for the why, who, and how of the intended change. If so, proceed to step 3. If an honest assessment of your leadership approach reveals a need to explore further support, then formulate a plan to provide the support.

3. **Select** the language and location to initiate the confrontation. Keep in mind that the language you use to initiate what the individual may perceive as an emotionally charged conversation will be critical to a positive outcome. Initiating the conversation with anger by saying something like, "What is wrong with you?" will more than likely not lead to the best approach. In addition, deciding where the conversation will take place may contribute to unwarranted anxiety. For example, a principal may choose to confront a teacher over a lack of follow-through on a desired behavior in his or her office, if the principal intends to do so in a formal setting. The teacher may perceive the confrontation as less formal, but still direct, if the exchange takes place in the teacher's classroom.

4. **Initiate** the tactful confrontation and then proceed to **Inquire** about clarification of the observed behavior or lack thereof so

you avoid articulating a misconception that may offend the individual. Seek to determine whether what you are observing has occurred due to a lack of skill ("I need more support to meet your expectations") or a lack of will ("I do not want to commit to your expectations").

5. **Select** the most suitable approach based on the information you gathered in step 4. If the reason the individual has not followed through stems from a lack of skill, then seek the most effective and efficient manner in which to provide support and verbalize your expectation before proceeding to step 6. If the reason the individual has not followed through stems from a lack of will, clarify that the desired behavior is not a request but an expectation, and proceed to step 6.

6. **Tell** the individual why and how you plan to monitor the desired behavior. If the individual will receive additional support for the behavior, outline how you will monitor progress. If you will monitor behavior due to lack of will, explain that the desired behavior is critical to the organization's success and, as such, you have to monitor the behavior until you trust it will continue without the need to monitor.

While we acknowledge that initiating tactful confrontation will require transformational leaders to lead courageously, we also acknowledge that when leaders fail to initiate required confrontation, they directly contribute to the organization's demise. In schools, those who refuse to directly and tactfully hold other adults accountable for communicated and supported behaviors are not leaders. Rather, these individuals are supporters of the status quo whose failure to demand full participation in a school's change and improvement process further creates a wedge between students and achievement (Muhammad, 2018).

In the following sections, we present three scenarios designed to help you practice your ability to get results. As you review and reflect on each scenario, we want you to critically analyze your current philosophies and practices. Ask, "Are my current theories and practices aligned or are they incongruent?" "Am I getting results?" Consider the research and evidence presented in this chapter to guide your answers and responses.

SCENARIO ONE: *Addressing a Negative Team Attitude*

You are beginning your second year as principal of an elementary school after having a very successful first year. The school had three different principals

DO!

in the five years prior to your arrival, which prompted you to "hit the ground lis-tening" to the staff's concerns prior to initiating any major changes. This approach seems to have paid off. The end-of-year teachers and staff surveys revealed 93 per-cent approval of your role as principal, the highest indication of trust in administra-tion in six years. In addition, your formation of a strong leadership team composed of well-respected and effective teachers allowed for honest discussions of data. This prompted the team to share with the faculty that all teachers had to place a stronger emphasis on core content knowledge (Tier 1 of the RTI model), "first best instruc-tion," for the upcoming school year. Hence, in your second year as principal, you will focus on providing teachers with professional development on effective collab-orative practices through the use of common assessments.

Four months into the new school year, investment in a "trainer of trainers" model seems to be paying off. Lead teachers from each grade level receive training on how to effectively collaborate with the expectation that they will then train their grade-level colleagues. Periodically, you and the school's leadership team remind the faculty and staff of the why behind this process and use data to show staff their significant (though small) strides in student achievement resulting from their effec-tive collaboration. Grade-level leaders report that training the trainers has created a positive buzz and enthusiasm for student learning. Unfortunately, one grade level seems to be struggling.

As you review the detailed notes that each grade-level team has to turn in after its collaborative time, you notice a pattern with the fourth-grade team. Periodically, team members are absent during the scheduled grade-level collaborative time. And on more than one occasion, team members have used their collaborative time to make copies of class worksheets—a behavior the staff agreed should not take place during the scheduled collaborative time. It particularly concerns you that the fourth-grade team's grade-level leader often displays a negative attitude at leadership team meetings and may project this pessimistic outlook to team members. When the leadership team reviewed the schoolwide student achievement data, it deter-mined fourth-grade students had the lowest evidence of academic growth. You find the perceived lack of commitment from fourth-grade teachers especially concerning given what the data showed.

How would you, as a second-year principal, begin to address concerns regarding the fourth-grade team? Should you initiate a confrontation with the grade-level leader or address the entire grade-level team? What course of action would you take next? Use figure 5.1 to reflect on this scenario and brainstorm strategies.

Scenario One: Addressing a Negative Team Attitude	Strategies
If you deem a confrontation necessary, what steps would you take to initiate this tactful confrontation?	• • •
What language and setting might you choose to initiate this tactful confrontation?	• • •
If you discover that the lack of follow-through is due to a lack of support of the why, who, and how (rational resistance), how might you respond?	• • •
If you discover that the lack of follow-through is due to a lack of will (irrational resistance), how might you respond?	• • •

Figure 5.1: Strategies for addressing a negative team attitude.

*Visit **go.SolutionTree.com/leadership** for a free reproducible version of this figure.*

Consider the following when reflecting on this scenario.

▸ While reviewing documentation to gauge whether or not implementation of a particular desired behavior is good, consider if actually taking the time to personally observe the behavior would be an additional step in the right direction. Would doing so provide additional clarity toward confronting the issue?

▸ Consider addressing the group leader prior to addressing the group to initiate a gradual approach toward confronting the issue. If the tactful confrontation initiated with the group leader is not sufficient, then proceed to initiate tactful confrontation with the group.

▸ Reflect on how this particular group has behaved before when expected to implement change initiatives. Has a negative attitude always been a characteristic of this group? Identifying patterns or a lack thereof may provide additional insight as to what exactly is happening.

DO!

SCENARIO TWO: *Confronting a Veteran Educator*

Becoming a counselor at your alma mater has been a dream come true, and when your colleagues nominated you to become the lead counselor, you could hardly contain your excitement and enthusiasm. Your former high school counselor, who is still, after thirty years, a member of the counseling department, is especially proud of you.

After reviewing data and meeting with administration, you decide that you need an action plan for more students to take the SAT. You conduct focus groups with students and discover that your department needs to better inform students of the steps required to get into college, because many students will become the first in their families to graduate from high school and attend college. You invite your colleagues to brainstorm strategies to address this issue. The group decides that once a month, counselors will present pertinent information regarding college admission, including information on taking the SAT, in classrooms. This way, they ensure that all students receive the information they require for postsecondary success. Because students are required to take four years of English, you approach the English department members to gain their support and permission to present your information during their classes. The English department agrees.

After three months of initiating this plan, counselors share positive feedback, and students report that they have much more awareness of the steps they need to take to access postsecondary institutions. At your next counselors' meeting, you ask your colleagues to share their experiences with presenting to students. It surprises you to learn that only one counselor, your former high school counselor, has not followed through with the agreed-on plan. When you politely ask your former high school counselor what happened, she shares that she has been too busy dealing with other counseling responsibilities and will present to English classes "when she has time." You sense disappointment from the other counselors that a colleague has not followed through with the agreed-on plan, but no one says a word to the veteran counselor.

You feel distraught over what to do next. Should you initiate a conversation with your former counselor about the expectations you, as lead counselor, have? Would it be rude to ask someone who was instrumental in your high school success to explain why she hasn't behaved in a certain way? If you choose not to address the issue, do you risk losing credibility in the eyes of the counselors who have followed through with the agreed-on plan? What course of action would you take? Use figure 5.2 to reflect on this scenario and brainstorm strategies.

Scenario Two: Confronting a Veteran Educator	Strategies
If you deem a confrontation necessary, what steps would you take to initiate this tactful confrontation?	• • •
What language and setting might you choose to initiate this tactful confrontation?	• • •
If you discover that the lack of follow-through is due to a lack of support of the why, who, and how (rational resistance), how might you respond?	• • •
If you discover that the lack of follow-through is due to a lack of will (irrational resistance), how might you respond?	• • •

Figure 5.2: Strategies for confronting a veteran educator.

*Visit **go.SolutionTree.com/leadership** for a free reproducible version of this figure.*

Consider the following when reflecting on this scenario.

▶ Accept the reality that failure to address behavior counterproductive to agreed-on expectations will reflect poorly on your developing reputation as a leader. Take time to evaluate whether or not you have provided sufficient support by not only reflecting on your leadership but also tactfully asking questions about how you could further support an individual.

▶ Remember that when transformational leaders confront others, they do so tactfully. Select the right vocabulary to generate a tactful confrontation. In this case, include the admiration you have for your former counselor as a vehicle for establishing a healthy tone.

▶ Be transparent and express how important it is that the team view you as successful for the sake of the department. Consider flipping the situation from what you expect to be done to the support you need to be successful. In short, consider doing everything possible to offer support as a means of generating the necessary compliance.

DO!

SCENARIO THREE: *Responding to Lack of Compliance*

Your credibility as a veteran biology teacher of twenty-two years has prompted your peers to nominate you as the science department chairperson. As the newly nominated chairperson, you are expected to work with other departments' leaders and administration to continuously increase your middle school's students' learning. At your leadership team meeting, you examine data indicating that within the past three years, minimal increases in student achievement have occurred. Rather than make assumptions about the cause of such poor student learning results, the leadership team decides each chairperson should explore possible sources of the school's low academic performance within their departments. Administration gives every chairperson a substitute to cover his or her classes for a day so that each chairperson can address this task.

You decide to spend most of this granted time observing colleagues from your department as they teach their students. Rather quickly, you make note of an interesting pattern: the majority of your colleagues use lecture as their only form of instructional delivery. As a result, students are often disengaged and bored, causing a disconnect between teaching and learning. You decide to create a professional development plan that includes all science teachers receiving one-day substitutes so they can engage in professional learning focused on what effective instruction should look like. You make sure not to single anybody out and instead use the pronoun *we* to address how to make necessary instructional changes. During this professional development day, you present teachers in your department with research-based effective instructional practices and demonstrate what these strategies may look like in the classroom. You check to see if everybody understands, and you receive an overwhelmingly positive response from your peers. To demonstrate their gratitude, each member of the department pitches in to buy you a gift certificate for dinner and signs a card thanking you for your efforts.

You feel satisfied with the training you provided; however, several weeks later, you revisit classrooms and are disappointed to discover that few, if any, teachers are using the strategies you learned together. What happened? Did you do something wrong? While you feel compelled to initiate a department meeting to gauge why members did not implement what they learned, you have second thoughts. Is addressing this issue more of an administrative responsibility? How would you, as department leader, address this issue, if you indeed should? Use figure 5.3 to reflect on this scenario and brainstorm strategies.

Scenario Three: Responding to Lack of Compliance	Strategies
If you deem a confrontation necessary, what steps would you take to initiate this tactful confrontation?	• • •
What language and setting might you choose to initiate this tactful confrontation?	• • •
If you discover that the lack of follow-through is due to a lack of support of the why, who, and how (rational resistance), how might you respond?	• • •
If you discover that the lack of follow-through is due to a lack of will (irrational resistance), how might you respond?	• • •

Figure 5.3: Strategies for responding to lack of compliance.

Visit **go.SolutionTree.com/leadership** *for a free reproducible version of this figure.*

Consider the following when reflecting on this scenario.

▸ Realize effective leadership is not only a result of things going as planned but also how leaders respond to perceived resistance to change. Do not doubt yourself. Consider tactfully communicating to the team the discrepancy between desired behaviors and actual results. Ask if what happened is a result of poor communication on your part.

▸ Consider returning to the data as a means of regenerating a sense of urgency for a second attempt at bridging the observed implementation gap. Understand that sometimes people need reminders of the why associated with the need for change.

▸ Realize that changing adult behaviors may require more than one initial attempt. Allow your perseverance to communicate to the team the need to embrace and implement the proposed change. Continue to explore numerous approaches you may take with your team until you and the team achieve success. Perseverance is addictive!

DO!

It is unrealistic for transformational leaders to expect that change in adult behavior will successfully happen on the first attempt. Effective leaders, whether extroverted or introverted, develop a courageous approach to ensuring goals are achieved because of communicated support (why, who, and how) and a relentless focus on the adult behaviors required for success. Therefore, while ineffective leaders may avoid uncomfortable conversations with others, transformational leaders tactfully initiate them if the process for progress so requires. Tactful confrontation is an approach transformational leaders must be prepared to utilize, as is professional monitoring of an individual's behavior that expresses an unwillingness to comply with articulated change initiatives.

Using Professional Monitoring

Whether the RESIST protocol for initiating tactful confrontation reveals the need to provide additional support (a response to logical resistance) or the need to hold someone directly accountable for actions he or she refuses to take (a response to illogical resistance), transformational leaders need to monitor behaviors essential to the organization's success. When doing so in step 6 of the RESIST protocol, they should commence with tact and mindfulness of established organizational procedures. For example, a teacher leader may learn that a fellow teacher cannot commit to an expected behavior because he or she needs additional support. In that case, the teacher leader may provide the requested support and even monitor the support's effectiveness without any pushback from the fellow teacher. However, if the resistance has resulted from the teacher's unwillingness to comply with an articulated behavior, regardless of the support (why, who, and how) provided, district policy may require someone with positional authority, such as an administrator, to commence with established monitoring procedures. Anthony Muhammad (2018) emphasizes this sentiment when he writes, "In many unionized states, this process is bargained, so the school leader must be careful to follow the mandated system of monitoring explicitly outlined in the master agreement" (p. 114). Well-intentioned transformational leaders must have cognizance of established organizational procedures related to monitoring others' behavior. Failure to do so may jeopardize the transformational leader's ability to effectively align behavior to the organization's desired outcomes.

Prior to exploring the ways in which transformational leaders may initiate monitoring for the purpose of organizational enhancement, we must first make a clear distinction between monitoring and harassment. *Monitoring* is defined as, "to watch, keep track of, or check usually for a special purpose" ("Monitor," n.d.).

Harassment, on the other hand, is defined as the act of creating "an unpleasant or hostile situation especially by uninvited and unwelcome verbal or physical contact" ("Harass," n.d.). While we realize that efficiently monitoring unwilling individuals may make them feel discomfort and anxiety (Muhammad, 2018), the objective of professional monitoring is to verify, without any doubt, the progress of human behavior that catalyzes effective organizational change. Moreover, while transformational leaders may meet negative attitudes and even unflattering remarks from the individual they monitor, at no time should transformational leaders resort to any form of harassment. DuFour and his colleagues (2016) support this understanding when they write, "Don't focus on the attitude—focus on the *behavior*. . . . Work that is designed to require people to *act* in new ways creates the possibility of new experiences. These new experiences, in turn, can lead to new attitudes over time" (p. 220).

Patterson and his colleagues (2005) recommend two approaches for following up with an organization's members who need direct accountability: (1) checkup and (2) checkback. The person with authority initiates checkups when it seems that an individual will likely accomplish little, if any, of the desired behavioral change without this form of continuous monitoring. Patterson et al. (2005) state that checkbacks are reserved for individuals who are "experienced and productive" (p. 211); in other words, they can be counted on to follow through. Considering that transformational leaders distinguish between logical and illogical forms of resistance in step 6 of the RESIST protocol, we conclude that checkups—what we refer to as *professional monitoring*—are the most effective course of action for individuals who willfully resist, either through words or through actions. The following list includes examples of ways in which leaders may initiate professional monitoring in educational settings. Please note that in each example, transformational leaders have already provided support in the form of why, who, and how, giving them no choice but to initiate the described course of action.

▸ A teacher refuses to use research-based instructional strategies that align with helping English learners. The principal directs the teacher to turn in lesson plans for weekly review that indicate which instructional strategy she plans to implement. In addition, the principal periodically visits the teacher's classroom and soon thereafter initiates an in-person meeting to provide constructive and positive feedback based on her observations. They engage in a conversation regarding additional support that she may provide to the teacher.

▶ A principal consistently fails to arrive to school on time and, as a result, is rarely present to welcome students and parents in the morning. The superintendent directs the principal to text her each morning when he arrives at the school site as evidence he has arrived on time. Upon receiving each text, the superintendent thanks the principal for being a visible resource for parents and students. After several weeks, the superintendent schedules a meeting with the principal to discuss how his visible presence as students and parents arrive to school has had positive outcomes on the overall relationship between school personnel and the community.

▶ Members of a high school's visual and performing arts and physical education departments feel that the schoolwide focus on literacy should not include their departments. The assistant principal overseeing these departments directs teachers to share lesson plans with him that include how they plan to incorporate the schoolwide effort to increase student literacy. Upon reviewing the lesson plans, the assistant principal offers both constructive and positive feedback and asks if he can observe the teachers' lessons and have a conversation with them afterward that may offer further support.

Each of these examples illustrates how a transformational leader responded when he or she had no choice but to resort to professional monitoring as a means of ensuring behaviors actually changed. Notice how the leaders provided individuals with feedback and offers for further support associated with professional monitoring; this is especially significant to this process. Overall, stakeholders should eventually view being professionally monitored as a supportive and positive experience. This sentiment may arise when transformational leaders take the time to discuss their observations of improvements that those they monitor have made.

While some may describe professional monitoring as a form of micromanagement, recall that these leaders needed to initiate professional monitoring because an individual directly refused to adhere to expectations after they provided support. We do not advocate that transformational leaders use professional monitoring as their first response to resistance, as doing so would violate the principle of balance between support and accountability, which chapter 1 (page 11) introduced. We simply advocate that transformational leaders accept the reality that when adults who work in schools refuse to implement research-based behaviors needed to increase effectiveness, they have consciously committed malpractice (DuFour et al., 2016).

Leaders who ignore this malpractice because confrontation or monitoring makes them uncomfortable have essentially aligned themselves with the malpractice. Muhammad (2018) captures this sentiment when he describes those who allow illogical resistance:

> Illogical resistance . . . will eventually call leaders into a battle of will. This is a fight that the school leader must win, because to allow [resisters] to operate in a school culture in the midst of effective transformation is akin to sanctioning the behavior. (p. 113)

In the following sections, we present three scenarios designed to help you practice your ability to use professional monitoring. As you review and reflect on each scenario, we want you to critically analyze your current philosophies and practices. Ask, "Are my current theories and practices aligned or are they incongruent?" and "Am I getting results?" Consider the research and evidence presented in this chapter to guide your answers and responses.

SCENARIO ONE: *Addressing Refusal to Use Best Practice*

As the principal of an elementary school, you recently shared data with the staff that indicated students have not demonstrated the learning necessary for them to be successful. Together, you and the staff researched best practice, which led you to decide to use common assessments to improve student achievement. You are disappointed to learn that a well-respected veteran teacher is unwilling to use common assessments with her third-grade team. This is especially disappointing because you recall that while the staff received training, the veteran teacher periodically called in sick and made excuses for why she could not attend makeup trainings. Additionally, the minutes from grade-level collaborative meetings continuously indicate that all third-grade teachers regularly analyze common assessments, except for the teacher in question. Conversations between you and the third-grade team leader revealed that attempts to support this teacher have been to no avail.

When administrators spent time observing teams engaged in collaboration, they came to consensus that third-grade teachers demonstrated knowledge of and engagement in common assessment use, except for the veteran teacher. You decide to initiate a tactful confrontation with this teacher. During your meeting, she expresses her frustration at not knowing how to use common assessments. Upon hearing this concern, you generously offer her support; she replies that she plans on retiring in a couple of years and asks, "Can't you just let this go?"

DO!

You immediately realize that refusing to hold this teacher accountable for a set of behaviors that all staff members have invested in and are demonstrating will send mixed messages to the remaining staff. It may even begin to erode the initiative's progress. How would you respond to the teacher's request? Would you initiate professional monitoring, and if so, how? Use figure 5.4 to reflect on this scenario and brainstorm strategies.

Scenario One: Addressing Refusal to Use Best Practice	Strategies
How would you communicate the need to professionally monitor desired behaviors?	• • •
How would you decide to professionally monitor this particular individual's behaviors?	• • •
If you discover that the individual needs additional support to learn expected behaviors, how might you provide that additional support?	• • •
What process would you initiate to provide consistent feedback on the observations you make as a result of your professional monitoring?	• • •

Figure 5.4: Strategies for addressing refusal to use best practice.

*Visit **go.SolutionTree.com/leadership** for a free reproducible version of this figure.*

Consider the following when reflecting on this scenario.

▸ Before initiating professional monitoring of behavior, consider answering the teacher's question regarding whether or not she may be excused since she soon will be retiring. Calmly explain why this expectation can't be overlooked. Even in the face of a person's unwillingness to comply with communicated expectations, transformational leaders must not deny an opportunity to return to the why fueling a particular change initiative.

▸ Do not forget to couple professional monitoring with support along the way. The onset of professional monitoring should not correlate with an end to support. Remember that the whole point of professional monitoring is to ensure compliance with desired behaviors. Accomplishing this goal will require continuous support.

▶ Remember that professional monitoring can include an array of approaches beyond actually observing the individual. For example, they include the collection of artifacts such as attendance sheets and, in this case, tangible common assessment data. Consider using a variety of approaches to professionally monitor behavior, and remember to offer both constructive and positive feedback, especially when the individual follows through with expectations.

SCENARIO TWO: *Checking Progress on Agreed-On Processes*

You are the principal at a middle school. Careful analysis of student data revealed that students from specific cohorts, mainly English learners and students with disabilities, were not progressing academically at an acceptable rate. The school leadership team began to explore reasons why these students did not excel. The team discovered that a lack of additional time and support at home significantly deterred learning. After several weeks of studying how more successful schools with similar student demographics support student learning and get staff input, the leadership team proposed changing the school schedule. It proposed that the school day include a forty-minute block of time when all students in need of academic assistance could gain additional time and support. After much discussion and planning, administration was able to create a thirty-minute block of time for this purpose, and 95 percent of the staff reached consensus to proceed with the plan.

Implementation of this plan required some patience and restructuring, but data have confirmed that the additional time and support helps students. The thirty-minute support schedule allows students to receive the extra support from teachers or other staff members whose instructional delivery of the specific lesson or topic has proven effective. It disappointed the leadership team to learn that three weeks after initiating this process some teachers refused to send their students to receive this help simply because they did not want to "share students with teachers who might confuse them." When administration attempted to explain that data from participating students showed the program's benefit, the handful of teachers who refused to take part filed a grievance with the teachers' association, noting the program violated their "academic freedom" as teachers. Even after leaders of the teachers' association indicated that they could not support the grievance because of the remaining staff members' overwhelming support of the program, the group of

DO!

teachers rarely, if ever, have sent their students for the appropriate support. Instead, they have chosen to have their students complete worksheets and do other busy-work that shows no indication that it supports learning.

You have scheduled a separate meeting with each of these teachers, and you anticipate they will each require a tactful confrontation that will ultimately reveal an illogical resistance to change. How would you initiate professional monitoring as a course of action? Use figure 5.5 to reflect on this scenario and brainstorm strategies.

Scenario Two: Checking Progress on Agreed-On Processes	Strategies
How would you communicate the need to professionally monitor desired behaviors?	• • •
How would you decide to professionally monitor this particular individual's behaviors?	• • •
If you discover that the individual needs additional support to learn expected behaviors, how might you provide that additional support?	• • •
What process would you initiate to provide consistent feedback on the observations you make as a result of your professional monitoring?	• • •

Figure 5.5: Strategies for checking progress on agreed-on processes.

*Visit **go.SolutionTree.com/leadership** for a free reproducible version of this figure.*

Consider the following when reflecting on this scenario.

▸ Upon preparing the language you will use and the location where this tactful confrontation will occur, be prepared to review with the person willfully resisting change a list of the support you have provided as a leader. Reminding resisters of this support may help the person to realize that his or her behavior is what made initiating professional monitoring necessary.

> ▸ Be very clear about the reason for professional monitoring of behavior and the manner in which it will unfold. Confusion of any sort may make matters worse instead of better.

> ▸ Be sure to articulate that professional monitoring of behavior will continue until you trust that the teacher will exhibit the desired behavior without the monitoring. Taking this approach communicates that the change initiative will continue for as long as leaders determine that the particular behavior is expected from teachers. This type of direct communication will convey to the person resisting change that there is no other choice but to follow through with expected behavior.

SCENARIO THREE: *Dealing With a Lack of Investment*

As the assistant superintendent, you have spent the entire year overseeing student learning and discussing with principals effective leadership practices that should increase student achievement. After participating in several book studies, attending conferences, and visiting schools with proven track records of student achievement, you and most principals reach consensus that if schools want to increase all students' learning, then they must involve teachers in promoting necessary changes and work with the staff as a whole. You collectively decide to formulate strong leadership teams at each school and outline the expectations for each team, which include characteristics of teachers who should be on the team as well as the number of teachers on the team (based on school size). These teams will support and influence staff members to embrace changes that could increase student learning.

As this plan begins to unfold, a veteran principal asks to see you about concerns regarding this new expectation. You are disappointed when this principal shares that he would find it difficult to create a leadership team because his leadership style aligns more with working solo than with working with others. In addition, he states that his experience as a successful retired U.S. Army sergeant is evidence of why you do not need to hold him accountable for a shared leadership model, as he had success with a leadership style of telling subordinates what to do. You take the time to review with this principal the research that confirms the importance of having teachers on a leadership team, and you explain that while you admire his time in the armed forces, school leadership may require a different approach. You offer this principal support to help him identify teachers for his team, and you reiterate that he can decide who is on the team and how he assembles the team, but not having a team is unacceptable. The principal leaves your office upset.

DO!

On the first day of training for principals and their leadership teams, you notice that the principal in question brings three teachers with him, fewer teachers than other schools of the same size bring. Over time, you notice very little follow-through from this principal's team, and after several school site visits, it becomes apparent that the principal is not invested in this important process. In fact, he does as little as possible to avoid having accountability. You schedule a meeting with him and intend to initiate a tactful confrontation. You anticipate, based on your observations, that the tactful confrontation will ultimately reveal illogical resistance to change. How would you plan to professionally monitor this behavior? Use figure 5.6 to reflect on this scenario and brainstorm strategies.

Scenario Three: Dealing With a Lack of Investment	Strategies
How would you communicate the need to professionally monitor desired behaviors?	• • •
How would you decide to professionally monitor this particular individual's behaviors?	• • •
If you discover that the individual needs additional support to learn expected behaviors, how might you provide that additional support?	• • •
What process would you initiate to provide consistent feedback on the observations you make as a result of your professional monitoring?	• • •

Figure 5.6: Strategies for dealing with a lack of investment.

Visit **go.SolutionTree.com/leadership** *for a free reproducible version of this figure.*

Consider the following when reflecting on this scenario.

▸ Consider that professional monitoring of behavior may need to include using your authority as assistant superintendent to colead the leadership team with the principal so that the desired results are not limited by the principal's lack of participation. This approach may further serve to communicate to the principal the fact that the use of a leadership team will happen with or without his participation, thus initiating positive pressure for the principal to comply.

▶ Continue to share with this principal the evidence that this particular collective approach toward leadership has proven to be successful in many schools and that the need to initiate professional monitoring stems from the research that dictates this is the right approach. In the same manner that we do not expect students to learn at the same pace, some adults may require additional time to understand and embrace certain desired practices.

▶ Be prepared to accept the fact that if professional monitoring of behavior does not convince you that a more positive attitude toward this collective leadership approach is established, you may need to use your authority as a district administrator to remove this principal. This is an unfortunate, yet real, possibility.

Conclusion

As we discussed in chapter 1 (page 11), organizational change is a challenging endeavor, especially for individuals who work in schools, and for some, it is a daunting task. Transformational leaders who face the challenge of altering adult behavior for the benefit of the organization must be prepared to deal with both rational and irrational forms of resistance to change. Moreover, transformational leaders must develop the skill set to initiate tactful confrontation by using the RESIST protocol to uncover the root cause of the resistance. If the perceived resistance is a result of the need for further support, then effective leaders will patiently listen to individuals describe the support they need to actualize the articulated change and align their efforts accordingly. However, when resistance to change stems from an irrational source—when the why, who, and how associated with the proposed change are made clear, but the individual still refuses to embrace the need for change—transformational leaders must proceed to hold these individuals directly accountable by initiating professional monitoring of behavior. This decision, while potentially uncomfortable, is necessary if indeed the desire to improve the organization is the ultimate goal. Use the rating scale in figure 5.7 (page 108) to rate your proficiency in getting results.

DO!

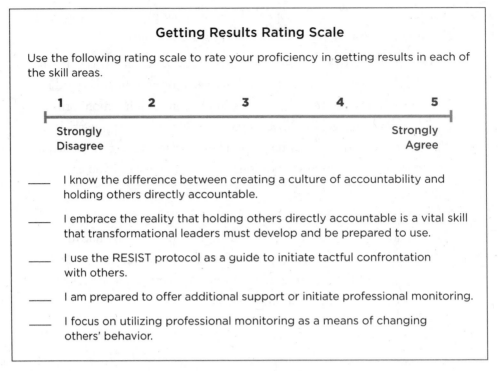

Getting Results Rating Scale

Use the following rating scale to rate your proficiency in getting results in each of the skill areas.

| 1 | 2 | 3 | 4 | 5 |

Strongly Disagree   Strongly Agree

_____ I know the difference between creating a culture of accountability and holding others directly accountable.

_____ I embrace the reality that holding others directly accountable is a vital skill that transformational leaders must develop and be prepared to use.

_____ I use the RESIST protocol as a guide to initiate tactful confrontation with others.

_____ I am prepared to offer additional support or initiate professional monitoring.

_____ I focus on utilizing professional monitoring as a means of changing others' behavior.

Figure 5.7: Getting results rating scale.

*Visit **go.SolutionTree.com/leadership** for a free reproducible version of this figure.*

6

Tying It All Together

We wrote this final chapter in August as we helped educators in schools and districts across the United States open the new school year with the focus and motivation they need to make a difference in students' lives. We reflect daily on the excitement and sheer energy that August brings, for educators as well as students. From city to city and state to state, we marvel at the eagerness and exhilaration that K–12 teachers and administrators exhibit as they take on the challenge to continuously increase all students' achievement. While hope and excitement fill this time of the year, the work we do with educators reveals the multitude of challenges associated with maintaining the enthusiasm of August for the remainder of the school year.

In many schools and districts, last year's state test scores become the catalyst for administrators and teacher leaders to launch efforts that aim to align teachers' and staff's behaviors with best practice and increase student achievement. Pressure to produce results that indicate increased student learning leads school and district leaders to conclude that school and district policies, practices, and procedures will require significant changes. As a result, in an effort to assist as many students as possible, leaders apprehensively launch movements that promote immediate change. For example, they launch movements to adjust teachers' instructional approaches or use more teacher observations that provide immediate feedback from administrators.

Over time, the pressure to change adult behaviors without a clear understanding of why change is needed; a lack of trust in who directs the change; and the absence of concrete skills for implementing the desired change will ultimately produce a sense of collective anxiety. This feeling will spread and soon morph into frustration that reveals itself mostly in informal school settings, such as in the teachers' lounge, in the parking lot, and even on Facebook. The frustration will rapidly mutate into misery and dysfunctional social interactions between professionals that interfere with the effective implementation of important policies, practices, and procedures designed to elevate student learning—what we call *adult drama*.

Some readers may think that the scenario we describe embellishes life in schools and districts. We can attest, based on our experiences with public school educators across North America with whom we have shared this scenario, that it is all too accurate. Is it any wonder that the same motivated public school educators we meet in August and September find themselves spearheading a desperate countdown to holiday breaks come November?

While adult drama regularly occurs in many schools and districts as a result of poor leadership, we do not blame well-meaning school and district leaders. As we have alluded to throughout this book, university courses and school district training place little emphasis on preparing educational leaders to successfully facilitate the array of behavioral changes that schools and districts may require. Over time, educational leaders' inability to successfully promote change in others will cement the notion that they are better prepared to manage adult behaviors found in schools and districts than to effectively transform them. If the goal of educational institutions is to increase student learning, then a transition from managers to transformational leaders is required.

In this final chapter, we discuss the need to understand the essence of leadership, follow support with accountability, and provide implementation tips for *why*, *who*, *how*, and *do*.

Understand the Essence of Leadership

If the reasons that prompt a state of collective frustration directly result from ineffective leadership, moving forward, educational institutions need a clear interpretation of effective leadership. While Google and endless academic research may introduce interested individuals to a wide range of definitions of leadership, we reiterate and expand our earlier definition of leadership through the work of three scholars. John C. Maxwell (2007), author of numerous books on leadership, including *The 21 Irrefutable Laws of Leadership*, rather simply defines *leadership* as the ability to "influence—nothing more, nothing less" (p. 11). Meanwhile, in their book

The Will to Lead, the Skill to Teach: Transforming Schools at Every Level, Anthony Muhammad and Sharroky Hollie (2012) describe *leadership* as the intentional act of increasing productivity for one's organization. DuFour and Marzano (2011) further contribute to the definition of *leadership*. In *Leaders of Learning: How District, School, and Classroom Leaders Improve Student Achievement*, they emphasize that effective educational leaders provide "teachers with the resources, materials, and support to help them succeed at what they are being asked to do" (DuFour & Marzano, 2011, p. 53). We combine these definitions of leadership with the skill sets we have described throughout this book that we believe transformational leaders need to effectively promote adult behavioral change. Because support must precede accountability for leaders to influence adult behavior to increase school productivity (student achievement), transformational leaders must provide those they expect to commit to behavioral changes with the resources, support, and materials they need to succeed at what they are asked to do.

In short, in this book, we have attempted to better prepare school leaders, both teachers and administrators, with the skills they will need to get others to think differently about proposed changes so that they feel differently and, as a result, are willing to do differently.

Follow Support With Accountability

As stated in chapter 1 (page 11), transformational leaders integrate into their leadership repertoire a clear balance of and distinction between support and accountability. Figure 6.1 (page 112) illustrates the dimensions of support and accountability we previously introduced, and then displays the four skill sets that transformational leaders must utilize within the context of support and accountability to most effectively facilitate adult behavioral change. Implementation of the skill sets requires transformational leaders to develop a keen awareness of when they must utilize particular skill sets. Although we advocate that transformational leaders must support organization members before they need members' accountability, organizations such as schools and districts embody unique cultures and circumstances that do not allow effective skill set implementation to always follow a sequential order.

Richard F. Elmore (2003) notes effective leaders understand that "knowing the right thing to do is the central problem of school improvement" (p. 9). Therefore, different school situations and circumstances may call for different, yet equally effective, approaches to addressing the why, who, and how required to successfully

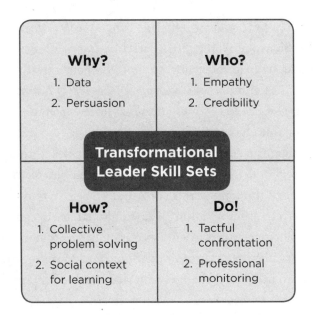

Figure 6.1: The Why? Who? How? Do! model and skill sets.

promote change. At one school, a stronger emphasis on establishing trustworthy relationships may precede any attempt at introducing the why and how associated with change. At another school, an effective approach may entail explaining the why and providing the how and, as a result, establishing stronger trust. In addition, the manner in which transformational leaders present data, demonstrate empathy, and involve their staff in the problem-solving process (all skill sets we have introduced that indicate support) may also vary from one organization to the next. Here, we therefore reintroduce each skill set we presented in earlier chapters and provide implementation tips that transformational leaders may find helpful in the implementation process.

The *Why* Skill Sets: Data and Persuasion

In chapter 2 (page 23), we proposed that transformational leaders consider the following actions when actively creating context as to why a school or district needs change.

- ▶ Use data to stimulate commitment to a cause bigger than oneself.
- ▶ Use data to create a starting point for improvement, not to scold.
- ▶ Use data as a tool to stimulate personal commitment and efficacy.
- ▶ Use context to persuade people to embrace an idea.
- ▶ Expect resistance and be prepared to respond to it without malice.

We emphasized that to persuade an organization's members to embrace change, transformational leaders must use data to influence others so they embrace behaviors aligned to the desired change. While transformational leaders certainly may use quantitative data to illustrate student academic performance and persuade a school's staff to embrace a proposed change initiative, we warn transformational leaders at all levels to cautiously avoid what Robert H. Waterman Jr. (1987) identifies as the DRIP syndrome.

DRIP stands for *data rich, but information poor.* Those who taught before the implementation of NCLB in 2002 might recall that they rarely, if ever, analyzed student performance data as a staff. In the accountability era (the 21st century), teachers and administrators view many bar graphs, data plots, and pie charts that indicate student academic performance—almost to a fault. If leaders present little to no context for statistics, it weakens the transition from data to persuasion, stalling desired transformation.

Richard DuFour, Rebecca DuFour, Robert Eaker, and Thomas Many (2010) emphasize this point when they state, "Data alone will not inform a teacher's professional practice and thus cannot become a catalyst for improvement unless those data are put in context to provide a basis for comparison" (p. 184). Scenarios such as the following may reveal possible DRIP outcomes.

▸ "I see that 29 percent of our third graders read at grade level, but this is good right?"

▸ "I see that our graduation rate is at 68 percent, but I am guessing this is better than most schools with our demographics."

▸ "I see that 67 percent of our students are eligible for free and reduced lunch, but what does that have to do with the fact that I still expect my students to complete homework assignments and for their parents to be willing to help them?"

In the following examples, transformational leaders use the same statistics along with context that supports the data.

▸ "I understand that 29 percent of our third graders read at grade level and that when we compare our performance with that of other schools in our district, we rank last among all third-grade teams. We may need to visit schools that have similar student demographics to learn what other staffs do more effectively."

> ▸ "I understand that our graduation rate is at 68 percent and ranks
>   well below our state's graduation rate of 87 percent. We may need
>   to create a team of teachers and administrators who can study what
>   we might do differently at our school to continuously increase our
>   graduation rate until it eventually matches and exceeds our state's
>   graduation rate."

> ▸ "I understand that 67 percent of our students are eligible for free and
>   reduced lunch and that our staff survey confirmed that 90 percent
>   of our teachers grew up in a middle-class or upper-middle-class
>   home. We may need to examine whether the manner in which we
>   experienced school fuels how we currently deliver instruction and, as a
>   result, makes it ineffective for our students."

There is a difference between simply seeing data and understanding the information that the data communicate. Each of the preceding examples demonstrates the clarity that data combined with context produces—a more compelling reason for staff to explore and potentially embrace change.

We have observed strong transformational leaders further create the right context to influence their organization's members to embrace change when they humanize data (Patterson et al., 2008). Transformational leaders humanize data by continuously, yet tactfully, reminding school staff of the moral imperative that led them to choose a profession that allows them to positively influence students' lives. For example, Principal Casey Ahner from Los Lunas, New Mexico, led Tomé Elementary School staff to commit to schoolwide change by coupling data with pictures of actual students (personal communication, July 13, 2018). This ensured that teachers and staff not only viewed data indicative of students' academic performance but also were reminded daily that percentages, pie charts, and graphs represented actual student lives. Over time, the Tomé Elementary staff sought changes in adult behaviors that led them to receive recognition as a high-performing school in the state of New Mexico.

Superintendent Zandra Galván from Greenfield, California, continuously reminds her staff that most students and families their school district serves are not simply eligible for free and reduced lunch but trapped in a cycle of poverty, and that all adults who work in Greenfield Union School District have a responsibility to "break them free" (personal communication, March 12, 2018). She and her team of both administrative and teacher leaders use this rallying cry to analyze data and explore adult behaviors they must embrace to better serve their students. To make sure faculty and staff always remember the purpose of their work, Superintendent Galván provides each adult member of her district with business cards stating, "I am part of an elite team dedicated to the arduous task of saving student lives!" Figure 6.2 features the image she uses on a PowerPoint slide to continuously remind stakeholders of the poverty cycle in which over 90 percent of Greenfield students and their families find themselves trapped, and figure 6.3 (page 116) shows a sample educator business card.

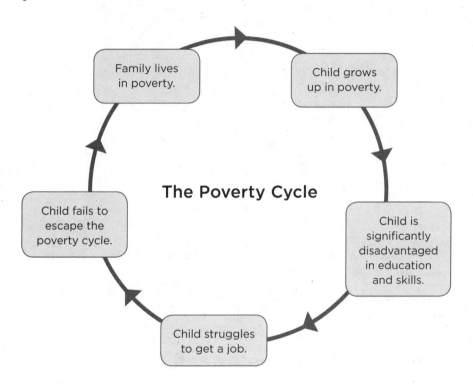

Source: © 2017 by Zandra Galván, Greenfield Union School District, Bakersfield, California. Used with permission.

Figure 6.2: Poverty cycle slide.

Transformational leaders effectively use data to not only inform adults throughout their school district but also, along with context and a basis for comparison, inspire and motivate them to seek and eventually commit to changes designed to increase student learning. We therefore add one additional reminder to the skill sets associated with data and persuasion.

▶ Couple data with context and a point of comparison to not just inform but also inspire.

Source: © 2017 by Zandra Galván, Greenfield Union School District, Bakersfield, California. Used with permission.

Figure 6.3: Sample business card for Greenfield Union School District faculty and staff members.

The *Who* Skill Sets: Empathy and Credibility

In chapter 3 (page 43), we proposed that transformational leaders should demonstrate the following actions when establishing trust so that they can initiate changes critical to the organization.

▸ Create opportunities to connect with and express deep concern about others' emotions.

▸ Listen, without rebuttal, to validate others' feelings, even if those feelings do not match your own.

▸ Collaborate with others to find a common resolution.

▸ Create opportunities to establish your core values and moral purpose and connect them to the values of those you lead.

▸ Create opportunities to demonstrate your deep knowledge, wisdom, and insight related to the proposed change.

▸ Prove that you have credibility by walking the talk.

While we stand by these actions as critical to transformational leaders' ability to effectively influence organizational behaviors, we realize that schools and districts also need to clearly identify who should become the transformational leaders who lead change. Our experience as public school educators and consultants has revealed a most peculiar assumption that educators make about school and district leadership: they falsely believe that leadership in educational settings is synonymous only with school and district administration. We appeal for a stronger focus on and a wider idea of transformational leadership in educational settings. It is not exclusive to school and district administrators but for any adults, especially teachers, seeking to change adult behaviors to increase schools' and districts' productivity.

Teacher leadership can have a powerfully positive impact in schools. Our experience as educational consultants with schools around the world has undoubtedly confirmed this. In fact, we've found that excluding teachers from actively participating in molding adult mindsets so they embrace behavioral changes that align with productivity simply creates a recipe for ineffectiveness and potential disaster (Muhammad, 2009). In *Changing Minds: The Art and Science of Changing Our Own and Other People's Minds*, Howard Gardner (2006) identifies positive peer pressure as an indicator needed to get others to think differently. Hence, who better to convince teachers to consider new, possibly uncomfortable yet necessary behaviors than other teachers, who can relate and have experienced similar challenges?

Equally essential to these particular skill sets of empathy and credibility, leaders must view leadership as not a singular but a collective endeavor. In short, focused and committed teams, not individual heroes, drive organizational effectiveness. These teams must include, at the very least, administrators and teacher leaders who work collectively toward common goals. John P. Kotter (1996) best captures this critical aspect of leadership when he states:

> No one person, no matter how competent, is capable of single-handedly developing the right vision, communicating it to vast numbers of people, eliminating all of the key obstacles, generating short term wins, leading and managing dozens of change projects, and anchoring new approaches deep in an

organization's culture. Putting together the right coalition of
people to lead a change initiative is critical to its success. (p. 52)

And while we have noticed that most schools have some sort of leadership team
on campus, traditional school leadership teams rarely focus on increasing student
learning but instead generally focus on topics more aligned to school management.
We therefore advocate for the creation of what Kotter (1996) refers to as a *guiding
coalition* (see also DuFour et al., 2016). In schools, a guiding coalition comprises a
team of administrators and teachers who continuously work together to embrace
the following three principles. In this way, coalition members build the necessary
credibility to influence others in the organization to embrace change initiatives to
do the following.

1. To guide and support staff members not on the team so they work
    together to continuously focus on increasing student learning

2. To learn, and then share with the staff, research-based best practice
    that aligns with increasing student learning

3. To actively listen to and provide a source of support for staff members
    grappling with challenging yet necessary change initiatives

The following list includes an array of purpose statements. Guiding coalitions in
schools in which we have worked developed these purpose statements for two reasons. First, to communicate to the staff from their schools the intention of the team,
and second to provide support to fellow members of their school community in the
pursuit of change initiatives sought to more effectively meet the needs of students.

▸ **Orange Glen High School, Escondido, California
  (www.orangeglenhigh.org):** The purpose of the guiding coalition
  at Orange Glen High School is to facilitate and share with our
  Orange Glen community the learning and implementation of effective
  research-based practices supported by relevant and meaningful data to
  ensure all students learn at high levels.

▸ **Naaba Ani Elementary School, Bloomfield, New Mexico
  (http://bfsdnaaba.ss19.sharpschool.com):** The purpose of the
  guiding coalition at Naaba Ani Elementary is to unify our staff
  by promoting a nonthreatening, mutually accountable learning

environment for all that recognizes and celebrates accomplishments along the way.

▸ **Nogales High School, La Puente, California (https://nogaleshs.org):** The purpose of the guiding coalition at Nogales High School is to positively unite and support all staff in embracing best practice to ensure an equitable, first-class learning environment for all.

▸ **Ochoa Middle School, Pasco, Washington (www.psd1.org/ochoa):** Ochoa's guiding coalition's purpose is to collaboratively inspire, support, and empower all staff and students to achieve at high levels.

▸ **Blackford Elementary School, San Jose, California (https://blackford.campbellusd.org):** The purpose of Blackford's guiding coalition is to guide, unite, and empower all staff to collaboratively take risks based on evidence of learning, mutual accountability, and best practices to ensure all students learn at high levels.

▸ **Southside Elementary School, Elko, Nevada (www.southside.ecsdnv.net):** Through support and mutual accountability, the Southside guiding coalition will unify the staff to promote best practices and undeniably ensure high levels of learning for all.

▸ **Pioneer Middle School, Walla Walla, Washington (www.pioneer49ers.org):** The purpose of the Pioneer guiding coalition is to guide, continuously support, and create shared staff accountability through the use of evidence-based educational practices to ensure that all students learn at grade level or better while celebrating our successes, both big and small.

▸ **Sharpstein Elementary School, Walla Walla, Washington (www.sharpstein.org):** As a guiding coalition, we aim to foster a community of learners who are passionate about promoting high levels of learning for all.

In addition to formulating a clear sense of purpose and focus as a guiding coalition, transformational leaders make sure that this team includes the right people who have the right attitude. Traditional leadership teams may ask for volunteers, a process that instantly has teachers drawing straws and hoping that your grade level or department does not choose them as the representative. But transformational leaders create a vision of the kind of leader the guiding coalition seeks and formulate a sense of honor and enthusiasm for joining this important team. Figure 6.4 showcases a sample application that clearly communicates the guiding coalition's purpose and the type of person the guiding coalition seeks. And while transformational leaders may open the application process to anybody interested at their school, they also seek out those individuals who can best fulfill the team's needs, and they actively engage in convincing these individuals to apply. Note that while we provide a sample application for your reference, with characteristics that we included based on our experiences, other transformational leaders may create one that better meets the needs of their school's culture.

Our good friend and colleague Mike Mattos often reminds school leaders, "If everyone is in charge, no one is in charge." Schools and districts that assemble guiding coalitions with a sense of purpose, noted in the previously provided purpose statements, position themselves to lead. They establish credibility with their staff for initiating change, and they establish the necessary support to positively impact the organizations they represent. We therefore add one additional reminder to the skill sets associated with empathy and credibility.

▶ Consider creating a focused guiding coalition and positioning it to establish credibility, practice empathy, and initiate change with the necessary support for educators to succeed.

The *How* Skill Sets: Collective Problem Solving and Social Context for Learning

In chapter 4 (page 63), we proposed that transformational leaders take the following actions to promote the necessary human capital and equip members of their organization with the knowledge they need to carry out change initiatives.

▶ Never assume people within the organization have sufficient knowledge and skills to effectively implement change.

▶ Create a vision of the organization free from the challenges it currently faces.

▶ Invite those expected to carry out change initiatives to discuss the problem and generate collaborative solutions.

Background

The fundamental purpose of our school is to continuously increase learning for all students. To accomplish this goal, both teachers and administrators must put forth a collective effort to achieve the following.

- Guide and support the faculty and staff to embrace that all students need to learn at high levels (grade level or higher).

- Learn and then share with faculty and staff research-based best practice that aligns with continuously increasing learning for all students.

- Continuously foster a school culture in which the faculty and staff passionately strive to increase learning for all students by analyzing data.

Eligibility

Our school's guiding coalition will be composed of both administrators and teachers who intrinsically seek to work with other adults on campus so they can continuously increase learning for all students. While all teachers and administrators are welcome to apply, the guiding coalition will include representatives from all academic departments and grade levels. Please note that the principal and a representative from the teachers' association will automatically appear on our school's guiding coalition.

Characteristics

Interested applicants must possess the following characteristics.

- Optimism in our quest to increase learning for all students (In short, a "Yes, we can!" attitude is highly desired.)

- Honesty and the ability to focus in on situations we, as a faculty and staff, can control when seeking to increase learning for all students, versus those challenges (such as poverty, lack of resources at home, and lack of academic foundation for students) we cannot control

- A desire to work with and assist other adults on our campus to reach their fullest potential as professionals

Skills

Interested applicants must be willing to develop the following skills.

- The ability to positively influence other adults on campus to think differently and thus do differently

- The ability to work with others to increase the productivity (learning) of the organization (our school)

- The ability to support faculty and staff members so they embrace and commit to change in policies, practices, and procedures aimed at increasing learning for all students

Interested applicants need apply by _____. Please submit a letter of interest detailing why you seek this position and what qualifications you possess that you feel will contribute to the guiding coalition's overall purpose, as described on this form. Please also include one letter of recommendation from any individual who can attest that you have the leadership skills sought for our school's guiding coalition.

Figure 6.4: Application for the position of school guiding coalition member.

Visit go.SolutionTree.com/leadership for a free reproducible version of this figure.

▶ Create a sense of empowerment and ownership in others to fuel the eventual implementation of new ideas.

▶ Formulate the appropriate social context that will allow learning to happen through interactions with others.

To intentionally create environments conducive to adult learning, transformational leaders must lead by example and embrace becoming lifelong learners themselves. In schools we visit as consultants, we note a distinction between leaders who continuously invest in learning with other members of their organization and those who do not. In Los Lunas School District in New Mexico, for example, Superintendent Dana Sanders attends every training that her staff have to attend, because, as she often states, "How am I supposed to support that which I do not understand?" Perla Rodriguez, principal of Echo Shaw Elementary in Oregon's Forest Grove School District, intentionally teaches summer school every several years (even though district administration does not expect her to do so) so she can stay abreast of the challenges and knowledge associated with effectively teaching students. This yearly experience allows Principal Rodriguez to not only strengthen her credibility as a transformational leader but also gain practical knowledge on how best to support teachers struggling to amplify learning in the classroom. Because she invested in learning how to become a more effective teacher, Principal Rodriguez has amplified her abilities as a transformational leader. With other teacher leaders, she has led her staff to achieve evidence of continuous growth for students from all backgrounds. To the surprise of no one who has worked with Principal Rodriguez, she was named Oregon's National Distinguished Elementary Principal of the Year in 2018.

Transformational leaders must seek knowledge and continuous investment in expertise in two distinct capacities: (1) the craft associated with teaching and learning and (2) the practice linked to effective school leadership. While teacher leaders continuously hone their craft due to the fact that they are still teachers, they can lead by example by continuously strengthening their ability to couple their teaching with evidence of learning, and then share their experience and findings with fellow teachers. In addition, all level leaders, including teachers and administrators, should spend time discussing, learning, and even practicing skills associated with, for example:

▶ How to use data with context to influence adult behavior

▶ How to build credibility by using empathy in their actions as leaders

   ▸ How to create environments conducive to adult learning

   ▸ How to initiate tactful confrontations

In short, transformational leaders embrace their role as lead learners and value human capital as fuel that can only strengthen their ability to effectively influence change in their schools and districts. Table 6.1 showcases some of the best internet sites that transformational leaders can access to further enhance their abilities as both educators and leaders.

Table 6.1: Resources for Transformational Leaders

Sites to Strengthen Educator Skills	Sites to Strengthen Leader Skills
• **Teaching Channel:** www.teachingchannel.org	• **The Education Trust:** https://edtrust.org
• **Education Northwest:** https://educationnorthwest.org /resources	• **Center on Great Teachers and Leaders:** www.gtlcenter.org
• **Annenberg Learner:** www.learner.org	• **The Edvocate:** www.theedadvocate.org
• **Underlined:** www.getunderlined.com	• **The Marshall Memo:** https://marshallmemo.com
• **Scholastic:** www.scholastic.com/teachers/daily -starters	• **Educational Leadership:** www.ascd.org/publications /educational-leadership.aspx

We therefore add one additional reminder to the skill sets associated with collective problem solving and a social context for adult learning.

   ▸ Invest in your own learning focused on critical aspects of teaching and learning as well as the skills associated with effective leadership.

The *Do* Skill Sets: Tactful Confrontation and Professional Monitoring

In chapter 5 (page 83), we introduced transformational leaders to the following actions that address individuals who demonstrate illogical resistance to change initiatives by professionally demanding compliance.

   ▸ Know the difference between creating a culture of accountability and holding others directly accountable.

▸ Embrace the reality that holding others directly accountable is a vital skill that transformational leaders must develop and be prepared to use.

▸ Use the RESIST protocol as a guide to initiate tactful confrontation with others.

▸ Be prepared to offer additional support or initiate professional monitoring.

▸ Focus on utilizing professional monitoring as a means of changing others' behavior.

As stated previously, initiating both tactful confrontation and professional monitoring may make both leader and follower uncomfortable, so transformational leaders must thoughtfully choose the best words with which to initiate this necessary, potentially charged dialogue. The RESIST protocol that chapter 5 introduced (page 90) emphasizes that a transformational leader needs to utilize the most effective vocabulary and setting when demanding compliance. But note that in this day and age, where more and more people secretly record emotionally charged communication, often in an attempt to control the narrative of a particular interaction, leaders should always be prepared to use the most professionally suitable language when addressing both illogical and logical resistance.

In his book *The Leader Phrase Book: 3,000+ Powerful Phrases That Put You in Command*, Patrick Alain (2012) writes, "The fact is no matter how successful you are, chances are your speaking and listening skills could use some polishing and finetuning" (p. 14). He then proceeds to offer phrases that leaders may use both positively and negatively under certain circumstances. Table 6.2 illustrates examples of both positive and negative responses that leaders may use or avoid in particular situations.

Due to the unpredictable nature of organizations and the complexity of human emotions and behaviors, transformational leaders will not always have the luxury to plan accordingly for each interaction they have. Therefore, it is critical that leaders at all levels frequently study and practice the manner in which they will address both logical and illogical resistance to change. In particular, they should emphasize the demeanor and vocabulary they use to communicate.

While being aware of phrases that could be perceived negatively is important, transformational leaders must also be cognizant of the role context plays in interpreting intended communication. Leaders should note the possibility that

Table 6.2: Tactful and Not-So-Tactful Language

Tactful Language That Transformational Leaders Use	Not-So-Tactful Language That Transformational Leaders Should Avoid
• "We appear to have a divergence of beliefs." • "I'd like to get your take on this." • "Did that answer your question?" • "That must have been hard to say; I appreciate your honesty." • "I am so glad we talked." • "I am sure we can get to a win here." • "Please forgive me if I've stepped on your toes; I did not mean to upset you." • "Please allow me to add one more thing." • "Only by working with one another will we succeed." • "May I tell you something in confidence?"	• "You're so wrong, you don't even know how wrong you are." • "Just spit it out already." • "That was my answer; take it or leave it." • "What gives you the right to judge me?" • "I am out of here." • "Wow, that's insulting." • "It's impossible to have a conversation with you sometimes." • "Hold your peace until I am done." • "Either we stay together or you get out of the way." • "What I tell you here dies here, OK?"

a particular response may work in one case but not another. For example, an employee who regularly communicates with and trusts a leader as opposed to an employee who rarely communicates with a leader and as a result has not established a trustworthy relationship would interpret the directive to "immediately come to my office" differently. Hence, while learning how to use vocabulary intended to establish a healthy dialogue is important, the role context plays in communication should not be underestimated. We therefore add one additional reminder to the skill sets associated with tactful confrontation and professional monitoring.

▸ Study and practice projecting the demeanor and choosing the words you will use when interacting with members of the organization while also being aware of contextual influences.

Conclusion

Our purpose for writing this book is twofold: (1) to formulate the idea that *leadership* is a verb, not a noun, and (2) to introduce transformational leaders to and better prepare them with the skills they require to address both logical and illogical resistance in educational settings. In other words, how leaders decide to act and interact with others will ultimately determine whether their organizations continuously improve or fail. We hope that the four skill sets we have introduced, along with specific actions and examples, better prepare leaders at all levels of education to channel the relationships they need to ultimately transform schools, districts, and educational centers around the world. With these skill sets, transformational leaders can help their schools and districts meet their highest potential in ensuring the welfare of all students.

Afterword: Final Thoughts

Public school educators find themselves facing the most challenging situation in their profession's history: implementing uncomfortable changes in adult behaviors that challenge the reality that the antiquated public school system was never designed to benefit the diverse student populations it serves in the 21st century. In addition, in the past, the design of the public school system commendably contributed to both agricultural and industrial economies. However, none of the educational system's original architects could have ever imagined that a global economy would evolve and require adults in schools to immediately change how they prepare students for 21st century success. More devastating to this real-life scenario are the consequences that educators' inability to embrace change will have on the students and families they serve, such as the following (Putnam, 2015).

▶ Fewer students will receive the preparation they need to become productive citizens, and as a result, more crime and bedlam will occur in communities around the world.

▶ Fewer students will rip themselves free from the stranglehold of poverty, and as a result, they will have more economic uncertainty and dependence on the government to meet basic needs.

▶ Few students of color will successfully win their battle against institutional racism, and as a result, more evidence of hate and division will spread throughout society.

▶ Fewer students will find their purpose in life, and as a result, they will have more negative experiences, generating stress and anxiety.

We have had the honor and pleasure of witnessing the powerful influence that transformational leaders have to change schools and districts for the better. But the truth of the matter is that not enough schools actively pursue and accomplish the transformation of policies, practices, and procedures that, when realigned, collectively create systems of opportunity for all students. We have written this book not to increase test scores but to launch a wave of transformational leadership in educational institutions around the globe that will ultimately make the world a better place for all people.

References and Resources

Accountability. (n.d.). In *Merriam-Webster's online dictionary.* Accessed at www.merriam -webster.com/dictionary/accountability on September 10, 2018.

Alain, P. (2012). *The leader phrase book: 3,000+ powerful phrases that put you in command.* Pompton Plains, NJ: Career Press.

Alicke, M. D., Braun, J. C., Glor, J. E., Klotz, M. L., Magee, J., Sederhoim, H., et al. (1992). Complaining behavior in social interaction. *Personality and Social Psychology Bulletin, 18*(3), 286–295.

Andelson, S. J. (2001). *FRISK documentation model: Practical guidelines for evaluators in documenting unsatisfactory employee performance.* Cerritos, CA: Atkinson, Andelson, Ioya, Ruud & Romo.

Anderson, M. J. (2007). Principals and conflict management: Do preparation programs do enough? *AASA Journal of Scholarship and Practice, 4*(1), 4–13.

Anfara, V. A., Evans, K. R., & Lester, J. N. (2013). Restorative justice in education: What we know so far. *Middle School Journal, 44*(5), 57–63.

Bandsuch, M. R., Pate, L. E., & Thies, J. (2008). Rebuilding stakeholder trust in business: An examination of principle-centered leadership and organizational transparency in corporate governance. *Business and Society Review, 113*(1), 99–127.

Bass, B. M. (1981). *Stogdill's handbook of leadership: A survey of theory and research* (rev. and expanded ed.). New York: Free Press.

Bass, B. M. (1985). *Leadership and performance beyond expectations.* New York: Free Press.

Bill and Melinda Gates Foundation. (2014). *Teachers know best: Teachers' views on professional development.* Seattle, WA: Author.

Boundless. (2013). *The nature of persuasive communications.* Accessed at http://oer2go.org /mods/en-boundless-static/www.boundless.com/management/textbooks/boundless -management-textbook/communication-11/understanding-communication-82/the -nature-of-persuasive-communications-395-1384/index.html on November 5, 2018.

Brown, J. S., & Duguid, P. (2000). *The social life of information.* Boston: Harvard Business School Press.

Browning, G. (2013, May 16). Why Steve Jobs' exactitude mattered as much as his vision. *Inc.* Accessed at www.inc.com/geil-browning/leadership-communication-structured -thinking.html on September 10, 2018.

Burns, J. M. (1978). *Leadership.* New York: Harper & Row.

Carnevale, A. P., Smith, N., & Strohl, J. (2010). *Help wanted: Projections of jobs and education requirements through 2018.* Washington, DC: Georgetown University.

Collins, J. (2001). *Good to great: Why some companies make the leap . . . and others don't.* New York: Harper Business.

Covey, S. R. (1989). *The seven habits of highly effective people: Powerful lessons in personal change.* New York: Simon & Schuster.

Covey, S. R. (2009). *How the best leaders build trust.* Accessed at www.leadershipnow.com /CoveyOnTrust.html on September 10, 2018.

Darling-Hammond, L., Hyler, M. E., & Gardner, M. (2017). *Effective teacher professional development.* Palo Alto, CA: Learning Policy Institute. Accessed at https:// learningpolicyinstitute.org/product/teacher-prof-dev on September 10, 2018.

Deal, T. E., & Peterson, K. D. (1999). *Shaping school culture: The heart of leadership.* San Francisco: Jossey-Bass.

Dizon, N. Z., Feller, B., & Bass, F. (2006, April 18). *States omitting minorities' test scores.* Associated Press.

Dougherty, J. (2013, December 13). The best way for new leaders to build trust. *Harvard Business Review.* Accessed at https://hbr.org/2013/12/the-best-way-for-new-leaders-to -build-trust on September 10, 2018.

DuFour, R. (2015). *In praise of American educators: And how they can become even better.* Bloomington, IN: Solution Tree Press.

DuFour, R., DuFour, R., Eaker, R., & Many, T. W. (2010). *Learning by doing: A handbook for Professional Learning Communities at Work* (2nd ed.). Bloomington, IN: Solution Tree Press.

DuFour, R., DuFour, R., Eaker, R., Many, T. W., & Mattos, M. (2016). *Learning by doing: A handbook for Professional Learning Communities at Work* (3rd ed.). Bloomington, IN: Solution Tree Press.

DuFour, R., & Fullan, M. (2013). *Cultures built to last: Systemic PLCs at Work.* Bloomington, IN: Solution Tree Press.

DuFour, R., & Marzano, R. J. (2011). *Leaders of learning: How district, school, and classroom leaders improve student achievement.* Bloomington, IN: Solution Tree Press.

Dweck, C. S. (2006). *Mindset: The new psychology of success.* New York: Random House.

Earl, L. M., & Katz, S. (2006). *Leading schools in a data-rich world: Harnessing data for school improvement.* Thousand Oaks, CA: Corwin Press.

Economy, P. (2015, May 22). 7 powerful habits for establishing credibility as a leader. *Inc.* Accessed at www.inc.com/peter-economy/8-powerful-habits-to-establish-credibility -as-a-leader.html on September 10, 2018.

Eller, J. F., & Eller, S. A. (2011). *Working with difficult and resistant staff.* Bloomington, IN: Solution Tree Press.

Elmore, R. F. (2003). *Knowing the right thing to do: School improvement and performance-based accountability.* Washington, DC: National Governors Association Center for Best Practices.

Evans, R. (1996). *The human side of school change: Reform, resistance, and the real-life problems of innovation.* San Francisco: Jossey-Bass.

Fullan, M. (2001). *Leading in a culture of change.* San Francisco: Jossey-Bass.

Fullan, M. (2003). *The moral imperative of school leadership.* Thousand Oaks, CA: Corwin Press.

Fullan, M. (2011). *Change leader: Learning to do what matters most.* San Francisco: Jossey-Bass.

Gardner, H. (2006). *Changing minds: The art and science of changing our own and other people's minds.* Boston: Harvard Business School Press.

Givens, R. J. (2008). Transformational leadership: The impact on organizational and personal outcomes. *Emerging Leadership Journeys, 1*(1), 4–24.

Grissom, J. A., & Bartanen, B. (2018). Principal effectiveness and principal turnover. *Education Finance and Policy*, 1–63.

Guisbond, L., Neill, M., & Schaeffer, B. (2012). *NCLB's lost decade for educational progress: What can we learn from this policy failure?* Jamaica Plain, MA: National Center for Fair and Open Testing.

Gumperz, J. J., & Cook-Gumperz, J. (2008). Studying language, culture, and society: Sociolinguistics or linguistic anthropology? *Journal of Sociolinguistics, 12*(4), 532–545.

Harass. (n.d.). In *Merriam-Webster's online dictionary.* Accessed at www.merriam-webster .com/dictionary/harass on September 10, 2018.

Hargreaves, A., & Fullan, M. (2012). *Professional capital: Transforming teaching in every school.* New York: Teachers College Press.

Harvard Business Review. (2011). *HBR's 10 must reads on leadership.* Boston: Harvard Business Review Press.

Hattie, J. (2012). *Visible learning for teachers: Maximizing impact on learning.* New York: Routledge.

Heifetz, R. A., & Laurie, D. L. (1997). The work of leadership. *Harvard Business Review, 75*(1), 124–134.

Herzberg, F. (1966). *Work and the nature of man.* Cleveland, OH: World.

Hurley, R. F. (2006). The decision to trust. *Harvard Business Review, 84*(9). Accessed at https://hbr.org/2006/09/the-decision-to-trust on September 10, 2018.

Kanold, T. D. (2011). *The five disciplines of PLC leaders*. Bloomington, IN: Solution Tree Press.

Keller, B. (2008). Studies link teacher absences to lower student scores. *Education Week, 27*(28), 9.

Ken Blanchard Companies. (2016, November 30). *Critical leadership skills: Key traits that can make or break today's leaders*. Accessed at http://images.51job.com/im /51newslettle/images/pdf_critical_leadership_skills.pdf on September 10, 2018.

Kennedy, M. M. (2005). *Inside teaching: How classroom life undermines reform*. Cambridge, MA: Harvard University Press.

Kettenhofen, C. (n.d.). *Empathy: A critical skill for effective leadership*. Accessed at http:// bouncebackhigher.com/articles/empathy-a-critical-skill-for-effective-leadership on September 10, 2018.

Kotter, J. P. (1996). *Leading change*. Boston: Harvard Business School Press.

Kotter, J. P. (2007). Leading change: Why transformation efforts fail. *Harvard Business Review, 85*(1), 96–103.

Kotter, J. (2010). *Eight steps for leading change*. Accessed at www.kotterinternational.com /.kotterprinciples/ChangeSteps/Steps2/Step2.aspx on January 10, 2019.

Kouzes, J. M., & Posner, B. Z. (2002). *The leadership challenge*. San Francisco: Jossey-Bass.

Kouzes, J. M., & Posner, B. Z. (2003). *Credibility: How leaders gain and lose it, why people demand it*. San Francisco: Jossey-Bass.

Lacey, C. (2012). *The socialization of teachers* (Routledge library ed.). London: Routledge.

Langston University. (2016). *Transformational leadership*. Accessed at www.langston.edu /sites/default/files/basic-content-files/TransformationalLeadership.pdf on October 22, 2016.

Lee, T. (2014, May 7). *Education racial gap wide as ever according to NAEP*. Accessed at www.msnbc.com/msnbc/student-proficiency-stagnant-race-gap-wide on September 10, 2018.

Lencioni, P. (2005). *Overcoming the five dysfunctions of a team: A field guide for leaders, managers, and facilitators*. New York: Wiley.

Levitt, S. (2017, March 15). *Why the empathetic leader is the best leader*. Accessed at www.success.com/article/why-the-empathetic-leader-is-the-best-leader on September 10, 2018.

Lortie, D. C. (1975). *Schoolteacher: A sociological study*. Chicago: University of Chicago Press.

Marzano, R. J., Waters, T., & McNulty, B. A. (2005). *School leadership that works: From research to results*. Alexandria, VA: Association for Supervision and Curriculum Development.

Maxwell, J. C. (2007). *The 21 irrefutable laws of leadership: Follow them and people will follow you*. Nashville, TN: Nelson.

MetLife. (2013). *The MetLife survey of the American teacher: Challenges for school leadership—A survey of teachers and principals.* New York: Author. Accessed at www .metlife.com/content/dam/microsites/about/corporate-profile/MetLife-Teacher -Survey-2012.pdf on September 10, 2018.

Miciak, A., & Shanklin, W. (1994). Choosing celebrity endorsers. *Marketing Management, 3*(3), 51–59.

Mineo, D. L. (2014). The importance of trust in leadership. *Research Management Review, 20*(1), 1–6.

Monitor. (n.d.). In *Merriam-Webster's online dictionary.* Accessed at www.merriam -webster.com/dictionary/monitor on September 10, 2018.

Muhammad, A. (2009). *Transforming school culture: How to overcome staff division.* Bloomington, IN: Solution Tree Press.

Muhammad, A. (2018). *Transforming school culture: How to overcome staff division* (2nd ed.). Bloomington, IN: Solution Tree Press.

Muhammad, A., & Hollie, S. (2012). *The will to lead, the skill to teach: Transforming schools at every level.* Bloomington, IN: Solution Tree Press.

Munro, A. (2005). *Practical succession management: How to future-proof your organisation.* Burlington, VT: Gower.

National Association of Secondary School Principals. (2002). *Principal shortage.* Accessed at www.nassp.org/policy-advocacy-center/nassp-position-statements /principal-shortage on September 10, 2016.

No Child Left Behind (NCLB) Act of 2001, Pub. L. No. 107-110, § 115, Stat. 1425 (2002).

Patterson, K., Grenny, J., Maxfield, D., McMillan, R., & Switzler, A. (2008). *Influencer: The power to change anything.* New York: McGraw-Hill.

Patterson, K., Grenny, J., McMillan, R., & Switzler, A. (2002). *Crucial conversations: Tools for talking when stakes are high.* New York: McGraw-Hill.

Patterson, K., Grenny, J., McMillan, R., & Switzler, A. (2005). *Crucial confrontations: Tools for resolving broken promises, violated expectations, and bad behavior.* New York: McGraw-Hill.

Peterson, P. E., & Hess, F. M. (2008). Few states set world-class standards: In fact, most render the notion of proficiency meaningless. *Education Next, 8*(3), 70–73.

Piaget, J. (1977). Problems of equilibration. In M. H. Appel & L. S. Goldberg (Eds.), *Topics in cognitive development* (Vol. 1, pp. 3–13). New York: Plenum Press.

Pink, D. H. (2011). *Drive: The surprising truth about what motivates us.* New York: Riverhead Books.

Putnam, R. D. (2015). *Our kids: The American dream in crisis.* New York: Simon & Schuster.

Ravitch, D. (2013). *Reign of error: The hoax of the privatization movement and the danger to America's public schools.* New York: Random House.

Reeves, D. B. (2004). *Accountability for learning: How teachers and school leaders can take charge.* Alexandria, VA: Association for Supervision and Curriculum Development.

Root, G. N., III. (n.d.). *Ten ways to build credibility as a leader.* Accessed at http://smallbusiness.chron.com/ten-ways-build-credibility-leader-20954.html on September 10, 2018.

Ross, L. (1977). The intuitive psychologist and his shortcomings: Distortions in the attribution process. In L. Berkowitz (Ed.), *Advances in experimental social psychology* (Vol. 10, pp. 173–220). New York: Academic Press.

School Leaders Network. (2014). *Churn: The high cost of principal turnover.* Accessed at www.acesconnection.com/blog/churn-e-high-cost-of-principal-turnover -connectleadsucceed-org on September 10, 2018.

Spring, J. (2001). *The American school, 1642–2000.* New York: McGraw-Hill.

Spungin, D. (2015, September 29). *Gaining and maintaining leadership credibility.* Accessed at www.linkedin.com/pulse/gaining-maintaining-leadership-credibility -david-spungin-msod-acc on September 10, 2018.

Stolp, S. (1994). Leadership for school culture. *ERIC Digest, 91.*

Sutcher, L., Darling-Hammond, L., & Carver-Thomas, D. (2016). *A coming crisis in teaching? Teacher supply, demand, and shortages in the U.S.* Palo Alto, CA: Learning Policy Institute.

Tavakoli, M. (2010). A positive approach to stress, resistance, and organizational change. *Procedia Social and Behavioral Sciences, 5,* 1794–1798.

Tyack, D., & Cuban, L. (1995). *Tinkering toward utopia: A century of public school reform.* Cambridge, MA: Harvard University Press.

U.S. Department of Education. (2013, August 29). *States granted waivers from No Child Left Behind allowed to reapply for renewal for the 2014 and 2015 school years* [Press release]. Accessed at www.ed.gov/news/press-releases/states-granted-waivers-no-child -left-behind-allowed-reapply-renewal-2014-and-201 on May 10, 2014.

U.S. Department of Education. (2014). *Civil rights data collection: Data snapshot—School discipline* (Issue Brief No. 1). Washington, DC: Author. Accessed at https://ocrdata .ed.gov/downloads/crdc-school-discipline-snapshot.pdf on September 10, 2018.

Waterman, R. H., Jr. (1987). *The renewal factor: How the best get and keep the competitive edge.* Toronto, Ontario, Canada: Bantam Books.

Waters, T., Marzano, R. J., & McNulty, B. (2004). Leadership that sparks learning. *Educational Leadership, 61*(7), 48–51.

Index

Overcoming the Achievement Gap Trap
Anthony Muhammad

Ensure learning equality in every classroom. Investigate previous and current policies designed to help close the achievement gap. Explore strategies for adopting a new mindset that frees educators and students from negative academic performance expectations.

BKF618

Transforming School Culture [Second Edition]
Anthony Muhammad

The second edition of this best-selling resource delivers powerful, new insight into the four types of educators and how to work with each group to create thriving schools. The book also includes Dr. Muhammad's latest research and a new chapter of frequently asked questions.

BKF793

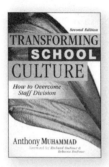

The Will to Lead, the Skill to Teach
Anthony Muhammad and Sharroky Hollie

The authors acknowledge both the structural and sociological issues that contribute to low-performing schools and offer multiple tools and strategies to assess and improve classroom management, increase literacy, establish academic vocabulary, and contribute to a healthier school culture.

BKF443

Learning by Doing [Third Edition]
Richard DuFour, Rebecca DuFour, Robert Eaker, Thomas W. Many, and Mike Mattos

Discover how to transform your school or district into a high-performing PLC. The third edition of this comprehensive action guide offers new strategies for addressing critical PLC topics, including hiring and retaining new staff, creating team-developed common formative assessments, and more.

BKF746

Solution Tree | Press
a division of
Solution Tree

Visit SolutionTree.com or call 800.733.6786 to order.

"Tremendous, tremendous, tremendous!

The speaker made me do some very deep internal reflection about the **PLC process** and the personal responsibility I have in making the school improvement process work **for ALL kids**."

—Marc Rodriguez, teacher effectiveness coach,
Denver Public Schools, Colorado